The White Stone

The Spiritual Theology
of John Henry Newman

Vincent Ferrer Blehl, S.J.

ST. BEDE'S PUBLICATIONS / Petersham, Massachusetts

Saint Bede's Publications
P.O. Box 545, Petersham, MA 01366-0545

99   98   97   96   95   94   93   5   4   3   2   1

Typesetting and interior and cover design by
Nighthawk Design, Grand Rapids, Michigan

LIBRARY OF CONGRESS CATALOGING-IN-PUBLICATION DATA

Blehl, Vincent Ferrer.
The white stone : the spiritual theology of John Henry Newman / Vincent
Ferrer Blehl.
    p.   cm.
    Includes bibliographical references.
    ISBN 1-879007-03-7
    1. Newman, John Henry, 1801-1890. 2. Spirituality—Catholic Church—
History—19th century. 3. Spirituality—Church of England—History—19th
century. 4. Catholic Church—Doctrines—History—19th century. 5. Church
of England—Doctrines—History—19th century. 6. Anglican Communion—
England—Doctrines—History—19th century. I. Title.
BX4705.N5B561993   93-31998
230'.2' 092—dc20   CIP

Those who give themselves up to their Lord and Saviour, those who surrender themselves soul and body, those who honestly say, 'I am Thine, new—make me, do with me what Thou wilt,' who say so not once or twice merely, or in a transport, but calmly and habitually; these are they who gain the Lord's secret gift, even the 'white stone, and in the stone a new name written which no man knoweth, saving he that receiveth it.'

JOHN HENRY NEWMAN

Contents

Abbreviations

Note: References to Newman's works are to the uniform edition 1868–1890, which was published by Longmans, Green, and Co.

Apo.	*Apologia pro Vita Sua*
Ari.	*The Arians of the Fourth Century*
Ath. I, II	*Select Treatises of St. Athanasius,* 2 vols.
AW	*John Henry Newman: Autobiographical Writings,* ed. Henry Tristram; London and New York 1956.
BOA	Birmingham Oratory Archives
Call.	*Callista: A Tale of the Third Century*
CS	*Catholic Sermons of Cardinal Newman,* ed. at the Birmingham Oratory, London 1957.
DA	*Discussions and Arguments on Various Subjects*
Dev.	*An Essay on the Development of Christian Doctrine*
Diff. I, II	*Certain Difficulties felt by Anglicans in Catholic Teaching,* 2 vols.
Ess. I, II	*Essays Critical and Historical,* 2 vols.
GA	*An Essay in Aid of a Grammar of Assent*
HS I, II, III	*Historical Sketches,* 3 vols.
Idea	*The Idea of a University*
Jfc.	*Lectures on the Doctrine of Justification*
KC	*Correspondence of John Henry Newman with John Keble and Others, 1839–45,* ed. at the Birmingham Oratory, 1917.
LD	*The Letters and Diaries of John Henry Newman,* ed. Charles Stephen Dessain et al., vols. I–VI, Oxford 1978–84, XI–XXII, London 1961–72, XXIII–XXXI, Oxford 1973–77.
LG	*Loss and Gain: The Story of a Convert*
MD	*Meditations and Devotions of the Late Cardinal Newman*

Mix.	*Discourses addressed to Mixed Congregations*
Moz. I, II	*Letters and Correspondence of John Henry Newman during his Life in the English Church,* ed. Anne Mozley, 2 vols., London 1891.
NO	*Newman the Oratorian: His Unpublished Oratory Papers,* ed. Placid Murray OSB, Dublin 1969.
OS	*Sermons preached on Various Occasions*
PPS	*Parochial and Plain Sermons,* 3 vols.
Prepos.	*Lectures on the Present Position of Catholics in England*
SD	*Sermons bearing on Subjects of the Day*
SE	*Stray Essays on Controversial Subjects, variously illustrated,* Private 1890.
SN	*Sermon Notes of John Henry Cardinal Newman, 1849–1876,* ed. Fathers of the Birmingham Oratory, London 1913.
US	*Fifteen Sermons preached before the University of Oxford*
VM I, II	*The Via Media,* 2 vols.
VRS	*Verses on Religious Subjects*
VV	*Verses on Various Occasions*

Introduction

WHETHER THE terms 'spirituality,' 'ascetical,' 'spiritual,' and 'mystical theology' have been emptied of real meaning is, I suppose, a moot question. In contemporary usage the term 'spirituality' describes 'those attitudes, beliefs, practices which animate people's lives and help them to reach towards super-sensible realities.' Hence, the term is not restricted to 'Christian spirituality.' The orthodox theologian Alexander Schmemann finds the latter ambiguous and would substitute for it 'Christian Life.'[1]

Louis Bouyer proposed that there is only one Christian spirituality; different 'Christian spiritualities' do not exist. On the other hand, spirituality can be defined as a personal vision of the truths of salvation with reference to a particular manner of putting that vision into practice. In this sense the great founders of religious orders—St Benedict, St Dominic, St Francis of Assisi, St Ignatius Loyola—had individual 'spiritualities.' These spiritualities need not, however, be equated with the particular ways of life institutionalized under their direction or inspiration. Various congregations, for example, were inspired by Jesuit and Dominican spirituality, but their rules and concrete way of life differ from that of the Society of Jesus or the Dominican order.

The terms 'ascetical,' 'spiritual,' and 'mystical' as applied to theology have different connotations. Ascetical usually describes certain exercises or disciplines designed to promote spiritual growth. Mystical refers to union with God on a level beyond the ordinary and characterized by special illuminations. Theology implies order, system, comprehensiveness, while 'spiritual theology' has been distinguished by Abbé Pourrat, the classic spiritual theologian, from dogmatic and moral theology as being 'above them but based on them.'

Since the Second Vatican Council it is increasingly difficult to maintain such rigid distinctions. Dominic Maruca affirms that medieval theologians formulated certain laws which governed the access to the summit of perfection, while contemporary spirituality in the Roman Catholic Church has complemented the earlier approach 'by introducing the implications of a renewed christology, pneumatology, ecclesiology, anthropology and eschatology.'[2] The present writer sees this as a return to a patristic model of theologizing, enriched by insights stemming from scriptural research and the so-called branches of theology. Newman follows this ancient model, anticipating in this, as in other ways, the teaching and spirit of Vatican II.

It is true that Newman never composed a formal treatise on spiritual theology, but the present work is based upon the conviction that his presentation of the truths of revelation and the manner in which they determine how one should live a Christian life constitutes, when synthesized, a comprehensive and coherent spiritual theology. How can one be sure, however, that the synthesis presented is not an artificial construct reflecting merely the personal view of the one who fashioned it? And could not a case be made for an equally valid alternate construction? The answer to these questions cannot be given at this point, since there has been no attempt to synthesize and coordinate various components of Newman's spiritual theology, even though some of the elements have been singly recognized.

Newman drew upon a tradition of spiritual theology in the Church of England, both Evangelical and High Church. Most Catholics, except perhaps converts from the Church of England, are unfamiliar with that tradition, its terminology, and its tone. In a number of sermons Newman refers to the aforementioned parties, though not by name. Consequently, when the main portion of this work was completed, the thought occurred, whether it would be necessary to see how Newman arrived at his spiritual theology. Obviously one could not write yet another biography, but it could prove useful to see what the influences of the Anglican tradition upon him were, and how in light of further study, meditation, and reflection he came to reject or modify what he originally embraced. Since continuous response to divine calls leads to an increased clarity of vision, it is necessary to see how Newman put into operation the principles once he embraced them, especially how he looked for, discovered, and successively responded to the will of God, for it is such responses that constitute the essence of sanctity.

The first part of the book, therefore, lays the groundwork for the synthesis presented in the major portion of the work, which will be more readily understood as having been anchored in Newman's personal attempts to understand and to live a Christian life, a life in the Spirit, a life based on a living faith in the Christian revelation as presented by Scripture and the Church.

Notes

1. 'Spirituality,' in *A Dictionary of Christian Spirituality*, ed. Gordon S. Wakefield, London 1983.
2. 'Roman Catholic Spirituality,' *op. cit.*

PART ONE

The Roots of Newman's Spiritual Theology

First Conversion

Born 21 February 1801 in Old Broad Street, London, John Henry Newman was the eldest of six children. Newman was baptized 9 April in St Benet Fink Church. Even today one still sees in print that he had a Calvinist upbringing or was raised in an Evangelical household. The evidence is quite to the contrary.[1] Newman's parents were conventional Anglicans, neither High Church nor Evangelical, and like most Anglicans of those days, they raised their children with a knowledge of the Bible and of the catechism. John Henry's catechism was quite sketchy. Sunday services in the church were attended and morning and evening prayers held at home. The children, however, received no formal education in doctrine.

Newman's grandmother and his aunt Elizabeth had a marked religious influence upon him as a child. They instilled in him a love of the Bible, but they also trained him. He called his grandmother 'his earliest benefactor,' and when she died, he wrote his aunt a letter filled with gratitude for what he had received from them.[2] In the *Grammar of Assent,* when he was trying to illustrate how one can have a 'real' apprehension of God, he speaks of a child's image of God before it had been reflected upon as a notion. The example is admittedly autobiographical. 'The child,' he wrote, 'may have but a dim shadowy sense of what he hears about persons and matters of this world; but he has that within him which actually vibrates, responds, and gives a deep meaning to the lessons of his first teachers about the will and the providence of God.'

A child's first apprehension of God, Newman continues, comes through the medium of conscience, not merely as a moral sense which tells him when he has done wrong, but conscience in its religious modality, for the child realizes he has also offended the Invisible person whose image he has in his mind, and he is moved to ask forgiveness of Him. Also the child has in his mind the image of an Invisible Being, who exercises a particular providence over him, who is present every where, 'who is heart-reading, heart changing, ever accessible, open to impetration.'[3] Finding God in conscience and trust in God's personal providence remained two fundamental principles of Newman's spirituality.

Of the early years at Ealing, where he went to school at age seven, little is known of his spiritual life. The atmosphere there was not particularly religious, and by age fifteen young Newman had deliberately sinned and fallen into skepticism. He confessed to John Keble in a letter of 8 June 1844 that at that age he was 'living a life of sin, with a very dark conscience and a very profane spirit.'[4] In his journal he described himself at that time as 'more like a devil than a wicked boy.'[5] Biographers and commentators have tended to dismiss this as a pious exaggeration common to saints and holy persons, but all the evidence would seem to indicate that Newman meant exactly what he said. For example, in *Meditations and Devotions* he confesses to having lifted up his hand against the face of Christ: 'Turn back in memory, and recollect the time, the day, the hour, when by wilful mortal sin, by scoffing at sacred things, or by profaneness, or by dark hatred of this thy Brother, or by acts of impurity, or by deliberate rejection of God's voice, or in any other devilish way known to thee, thou has struck The All-holy One.'[6]

It is difficult to see how this confession would apply to Newman at any time after his first conversion. The use of the term 'devilish,' moreover, tends to confirm the previous reference to his earlier life. But there is confirmation also in some of his verses on his Guardian Angel: 'And when, ere boyhood yet was gone, / My rebel spirit fell, / Oh! thou didst see, and shudder too, / Yet bear each deed of hell.'[7] He was, if not in a state of unbelief, at least in one of skepticism. In a letter to Sr Mary Imelda Poole in 1856, he wrote, 'I was at Bridgewater, forty years ago next July an ungodly, unbelieving boy of 15.'[8]

On several occasions Newman describes a boy who had hitherto, despite transgressions, respected the authority of conscience, but upon emerging into youth deliberately sins and falls from religious practice into unbelief or skepticism. The gradual transgression of the first commandment of the Law, he continues, 'is generally attended by a transgression of the fifth.' In this passage and in a similar one, he describes how this leads to a loss of enjoyment of one's home and family circle: 'His curiosity now takes a new turn; he listens to views and discussions which are inconsistent with the sanctity of religious faith. . . . As time goes on, however, living with companions who have no fixed principles . . . or worse, hearing or reading what is directly against religion, at length, without being conscious of it, he admits a sceptical influence upon his mind. . . . he does not recognize it . . . till some day suddenly, from some accident, the fact breaks upon him, and he sees clearly that he is an unbeliever himself.'[9]

Another indication that this is autobiographical is his affirmation that such an experience leads to a loss of enjoyment of one's home and family circle. In the verses, 'Mortal Sin,' he writes that 'I sought awhile / The scenes I prized before; / But parent's praise and sister's smile / Stirred my cold heart no more.' Several other sets of verses, 'The Stains of Sin' 'The Wounds of Sin,' and 'The Scars of Sin,' make reference to this youthful encounter with sin.[10] As will be seen in detail, Newman placed a certain emphasis on the effects especially of youthful sins upon the personality and character of the offender.

In March 1816 following the end of the Napoleonic wars Newman's father's bank stopped payments. John remained at school during the summer while his parents let the London Southampton house and moved to Alton. It was during this summer that John Henry fell ill, the first of three illnesses which were accompanied by intense spiritual experiences. 'The first keen, terrible one, when I was a boy of 15,' he later wrote, 'and it *made me a Christian*—with experiences before and after, awful, and known only to God.'[11] This is another indication that he did not consider himself a Christian at the time.

Mr. Walter Mayers, a master at the School who became Newman's spiritual guide, put into his hands various Evangelical writers. Though these authors played a role in his conversion, his was not an Evangelical conversion as that experience is described by them in their writings. For one thing, it was not a sudden conversion, as commonly asserted by Evangelicals, but lasted for five months, from August to December 1816, as he himself stated. Although he later acknowledged, 'I was terrified under the heavy hand of God,' he also insisted, 'my feelings were not *violent*, but a returning to, a renewing of, principles, under the Holy Spirit, which I had *already* felt, and in a measure acted on, when young.'[12] The conversion was, moreover, an intellectual one, since it gave him certitude of God's existence, 'as cutting at the root of doubt, providing a chain between the soul and God.'[13] The skepticism or disbelief into which he had fallen was eradicated and wiped out. Moreover, the experience touched his affections, in fact, his entire being: 'Thou didst change my heart, and in part my whole mental complexion at that time.'[14] So he insisted this conversion was not merely 'a reforming'; 'I know and am sure that before I was blind, but now I see.' Later he would also recognize it as a great act of God's providence.[15]

On 17 November 1817, two weeks before he received Holy Communion for the first time, he wrote a prayer of gratitude: '. . . whereas I was proud, self-righteous, impure, abominable, Thou was pleased to turn me to thee from such a state of darkness and irreligion, by a mercy which is too wonderful for me, and make me fall down humbled and abased before Thy foot-stool.'[16]

One of the writers to whom Mayers introduced Newman was Thomas Scott of Aston Sandford. To him, Newman wrote in the *Apologia*, '(humanly speaking) I almost owe my soul.' His book, the *Force of Truth*, described his spiritual journey in quest of religious truth from Unitarianism to belief in the Trinity. Newman was immediately attracted to what he termed 'his bold unworldliness and vigorous independence of mind. He followed truth wherever it led him.' That truth and holiness were both a quest and a development was summed up for Newman in two sayings of Scott: 'Holiness rather than peace,' and 'Growth, the only evidence of life.'[17] Moreover, he attested that it was Scott who first implanted in his mind the fundamental truth of the Trinity. In a subsequent passage in the *Apologia* he affirmed that 'from the age of fifteen, dogma has been the fundamental principle of my religion.' Spirituality without a foundation in dogma was henceforth incomprehensible to him: 'I cannot enter into the idea of any other sort of religion; religion, as a mere sentiment, is to me a dream and a mockery. As well can there be filial love without the fact of a father, as devotion without the fact of a Supreme Being.'[18] Newman later gave a fuller explanation of this fundamental principle when exploring the question of the development of doctrine.[19]

Newman also read William Romaine, another Evangelical author, from whom he learned the doctrine of election to eternal glory, a doctrine which he now took up, but which faded away with time. For the moment, however, it tended to confirm him in his early mistrust of the reality of material phenomena, 'making me rest,' he said, 'in the thought of two and two only absolute and luminously self-evident beings, myself and my Creator.' This is one of those frequently quoted passages of the *Apologia*. It has been used by some commentators and indeed his opponents during his lifetime to show that he was a recluse, autocentric. That it did isolate him to some extent was true, but he never became a recluse or antisocial.[20]

Another work which had a profound effect upon the young Newman was Joseph Milner's *History of the Church of Christ* (1794), for it introduced him to the world of the Fathers of the Church, an interest that developed in time when he was able to explore them in depth. At the moment he was 'enamoured of the long extracts from St Augustine, St Ambrose, and the Fathers' he found there.[21]

At this time too Newman had what he called 'an anticipation,' which he reluctantly mentioned in the *Apologia,* that it would be God's will that he lead a single life. This anticipation remained almost unbroken until 1829, after which there was no break at all. It was connected in his mind, he said, with the conviction that a single life would be required by whatever he chose to do in his life.[22] In a draft version of the passage in the *Apologia,* he was more specific regarding this vocation: 'This imagination . . . was not founded on the Catholic belief of the moral superiority of the single life over the married, which I did not hold till many years afterwards when I was taught it by Hurrell Froude. It arose from my feeling of separation from the visible world, and it was connected with a notion that my mission in life would require such a sacrifice as it involved. When I was first on the Oriel foundation, it was associated in my mind with Missionary employment, or with duties in Oxford.'[23]

It would take years before Newman put into theological perspective the significance of this conversion experience, but in addition to the effects mentioned, he was to become, to use a phrase frequently employed by the writers he read and one used by himself in his early sermons, 'a religious inquirer' as well as a pursuer of holiness, for the two were intimately linked. The first stirrings of theological inquiry can be observed in a letter to Mr Mayers thanking him for the gift of Beveridge's *Private Thoughts*. In the letter Newman complains that there is a passage which he does not completely understand, and that even before he had read it, he had debated within himself 'how it could be that baptized infants, dying in infancy, could be saved, unless the Spirit of God was given them; which seems to contradict the opinion that *baptism* is not accompanied by the Holy Ghost.'[24] The doctrine of the need for universal conscious conversion with the concomitant denial of what was called 'baptismal regeneration' had practically become the touchstone of Evangelical orthodoxy. Mr Mayers' explanation evidently satisfied Newman at the time, though later he would come to accept baptismal regeneration.

Though William Beveridge's *Private Thoughts* is not mentioned in the *Apologia* because it did not influence his religious opinions, nevertheless, 'no book was more dear to me,' he later wrote, 'or exercised a more powerful influence over my devotion and my habitual thoughts. In my private memoranda I ever wrote in its style.'[25] Joseph Bacchus called the work 'a solid treatise on the duties of a Christian life. It is severe in its tone, and makes no appeal to the imagination or to the emotions. . . . It speaks much for the maturity of Newman's religious life when he was only sixteen, that such a book should have captivated him.'[26] It preached the 'stern necessity of self-denial,' and it may be that its vision of the Christian life as a spiritual warfare explains Newman's predilection for military imagery and metaphors.

Someone reading Newman's journals without previous acquaintance with any of his other writings is likely to be repelled precisely by reason of its style imitative of Beveridge. Newman himself recognized this, and explained it by saying, 'I seldom wrote without an eye to style, and since my taste was bad, my style was bad. . . . Also my Evangelical tone contributed to its bad taste.'[27]

As a result of his readings and spiritual experience Newman mapped out a program for growth in sanctity. It consisted in daily reading of the Scriptures, prayer, self-examination, and later devout and frequent reception of the Eucharist. He resolved to be detached from the world. During his undergraduate years at Trinity College, Oxford, he continued to struggle against worldliness and while preparing for his final examination, he prayed that he would receive no honors if it meant that he would thereby sin. His failure to take honors in the Schools he accepted as an act of God's providence.[28]

Returning to Oxford in February 1821, he read William Wilberforce's *Practical Christianity* and resolved no longer to attend the theater of his own accord. He spent the following summer summarizing on paper his Evangelical beliefs. He also set down a description of the classical Evangelical conversion in the language of the books, but was somewhat surprised to realize that the description did not fit his own conversion experience.[29]

Newman's journals reveal his earnest endeavors to lead a spiritual life and to overcome what he considered his main sins and defects, especially pride, vanity, ambitiousness, anger (toward his brother Frank in particular), contentiousness, and ill-temper.[30] He also records having bad thoughts and his efforts to turn away from them. In the draft of the *Apologia* he remarks that he 'had a strong persuasion that offences against the rule of purity were each of them visited sharply and surely from above.'[31] For this reason he was distressed at the thought of going to dances or the theater. Like most persons who strive to live a prayerful life he experienced distractions in prayer. Spiritual affections would often be aroused by reading spiritual books, and he could pray on his solitary walks, but come the appointed hour for devotion he 'was cold and dead,' 'a dreadful listlesness comes over me morning after morning and evening after evening.'[32] In August 1821 he began to take Holy Communion every fortnight. Frequent communion was not usual in the Church of England except among the Evangelicals, and his mother objected, thinking he was beginning 'to be righteous overmuch, and was verging upon enthusiasm.' He practiced self-examination especially before reception of the Eucharist.[33] In 1823 he began to memorize large portions of the Bible, including whole books.[34]

Newman's Evangelicalism brought him in conflict at times with his father. He supported his brother Frank's refusal to copy one of his father's letters on Sunday. This led to a painful scene, but reconciliation followed. Concerned, however, by the effects of his son's beliefs and emotions on his nerves, Newman's father issued a stern warning against intensity in religious belief. His opinions would surely change in time. John Henry was convinced they would not.[35]

In 1823 Newman was elected fellow of Oriel College and struck up a spiritual friendship with Edward Bouverie Pusey, at whose suggestion he accepted the curacy of St Clement's, Oxford. He was ordained deacon in June 1824. Ordination was a deep emotional and spiritual experience. He was overwhelmed at the meaning of the vow, 'I have responsibility of souls on me to the day of my death.'[36] Not only was he never to lose this sense of responsibility and dedication, but it was to increase and to manifest itself in an acute concern for the spiritual welfare of the Church which he came to view as in a state of crisis.

In Pursuit of Truth: A Change of View

While discharging his duties in the parish with remarkable pastoral energy and zeal, visiting each family with concern for their spiritual welfare, Newman began at the same time to question and then to surrender certain Evangelical principles. The catalyst of the change was a fellow of Oriel and Curate of St Mary's, Edward Hawkins, who criticized Newman's first sermon, 'Man goeth forth to his work and to his labors until evening,' on the ground of an implied denial of baptismal rebirth or regeneration. It divided Christians into two rigid classes: those who belong to Christ and those who do not. 'Men are not either saints or sinners; but they are not so good as they should be, and better than they might. . . . Preachers should follow the example of St Paul; *he* did not divide his brethren into two, the converted and the unconverted, but he addressed them all as "in Christ" . . . and this, while he was rebuking them for irregularities and scandals which had occurred among them.' Newman's pastoral experience confirmed what Hawkins predicted, that Calvinism 'would not work in a parish, it was unreal.'[37]

Hawkins gave him John Bird Sumner's *Apostolical Preaching* which 'was successful beyond any thing else in rooting out evangelical doctrines' from his creed. Richard Whately, who exercised a great intellectual influence on Newman, also contributed to this change. At first Newman was sorely perplexed and prayed for light. He records in his journal: 'I think I really desire the truth, and would embrace it, wherever I found it.' Moreover, composing sermons forced him to order his ideas, and he began to realize that he had taken 'many doctrines on trust from Scott etc and on serious examination hardly find them confirmed by Scripture.'[38]

There was another principle which Newman acknowledges as having learned from Hawkins, that of tradition. Scripture was never intended to teach doctrine, but only to prove it, and 'that, if we would learn doctrine, we must have recourse to the formularies of the Church; for instance to the Catechism, and to the Creeds.' He considers that, after learning from them the doctrines of Christianity, the inquirer must verify them by Scripture. This struck at the foundation of the Bible Society, an Evangelical organization of which Newman was a member and which he later tried to reform.[39] He also came to criticize the Evangelical use of Scripture. 'Instead of attempting to harmonize Scripture with Scripture,' he said, 'much less referring to Antiquity to enable them to do so, they either drop altogether, or explain away, whole portions of the Bible.' The rich and varied revelation of Christ is practically reduced to a few chapters of St Paul's Epistles.[40]

What is evident in these changes is the expansion of Newman's views on revelation to include far more than his limited Evangelical views. The study of the Fathers would expand even further and deepen this vision of the truths of revelation.

On Trinity Sunday 1825 Newman was ordained priest. It would take some time before he accepted baptismal regeneration, and for years 'certain shreds and tatters' of Evangelical doctrine hung about his preaching. This was particularly true with regard to a series of sermons preached at St Mary's in 1829 on the Epistle to the Romans, and more precisely in his Evangelical understanding of such terms as 'justification,' 'faith,' and 'justification by faith alone.' Evangelicals separated 'justification,' and instantaneous act, from regeneration, or sanctification, which was progressive. Justification, for example, remains extrinsic or imputed. God declares man justified and treats him as such, though intrinsically he remains a sinner. Not until later, in the mid-1830s, did Newman come to accept a justification that is intrinsic, identified with regeneration, produced by the Holy Spirit, not from without, but dwelling in the soul, a holiness first imparted in baptism but capable of development over a lifetime.[41] Moreover, he did not separate himself from such Evangelical groups as the Missionary and Bible Societies until 1830, thinking that by remaining he could lead them to more ecclesial principles.

What, then, did Newman retain from his Evangelicalism? In addition to his habits of prayer and devotion he retained from his Evangelical mentors the view that holiness is necessary for salvation, but that it is not natural to man. Hence he must undergo a conversion, a total *metanoia* of his whole being. Though he changed his view of the nature of conversion and of regeneration or sanctification, he continued to accept and later to preach 'holiness the end of life.' The first sermon in volume 1 of the *Parochial and Plain Sermons* is entitled 'Holiness necessary for future blessedness,' a rewrite of a sermon composed when he was an Evangelical, but the theme is repeated in other later sermons: 'None but the holy can look upon the Holy One; without holiness no man can endure to see the Lord.'[42]

The great obstacle to holiness is sin. The second great obstacle is 'worldliness,' not only insofar as it is sinful but in the pursuit of earthly desires, ambitions, and satisfactions to the neglect of the primary purpose of life ordained by God. Newman retained the conviction too that there was a great difference between the 'nominal' and 'real' Christian, and that many, perhaps the majority, who claimed to be Christian were so only in name.[43] This distinction was popularized by William Wilberforce, the emancipator of the slaves, in his work, *A Practical View of the Prevailing Religious System of Professed Christians in the Upper Classes,* though Beveridge and William Law had also made the distinction.[44]

Oriel Tutor: The Drift toward Liberalism

In January 1826 Newman accepted an offer to become a tutor at Oriel. Since he believed his vocation lay in teaching rather than in parish work, he resigned his curacy at Clement's 21 February. He undertook the tutorship 'with a clear view of it as a pastoral and religious duty, not simply as a secular office.' Hating 'the martinet manner then in fashion with college tutors,' he cultivated relations of friendship with his own pupils, who in turn responded with affection and hard work. He began to have an influence not only on their academic life, but on their religious life as well, though more by example than by indoctrination.[45] His letters to his mother and sisters reveal that he was caught up in the doings of the College. Earlier thoughts of a missionary vocation seem to have faded away, replaced by those related to an academic future. On 21 February, 1827 in his annual review of the previous year he speaks of having become worldly: 'thoughts about livings, the Provostship, promotions, etc. come before my mind. I am remiss in private prayer, and reading the Scriptures. . . . I am not aware of any Christian grace I have grown in.'[46]

As he later came to realize, he was in fact drifting in the direction of 'liberalism,' and beginning to prefer intellectual excellence to moral. He began to think of the Trinity in a way that tended toward Arianism, without recognizing it (e.g., in a sermon preached on the mediatorial Kingdom of Christ, 15 April 1827). He criticized the Athanasian Creed as 'unnecessarily scientific.' He admitted to a certain disdain for antiquity, exhibited 'in some flippant language against the Fathers,' in his article on miracles. He rejected a number of miracles as being incompatible with God's wisdom. He was rudely awakened by two blows: illness and bereavement.[47]

Overly concerned about the responsibility of being a Public Examiner in the Schools, he had read seven or eight hours a day during the long vacation of 1827. At the end of November he collapsed while examining in the schools. Convalescing at Brighton his thoughts were filled with the forthcoming election of a new Provost of Oriel, in which he preferred the practical-minded Hawkins to the 'angelic' Keble, who withdrew his candidature. In the meantime on 5 January 1828 his sister Mary died suddenly at the age of nineteen. 'She was gifted,' wrote Newman, 'with that singular sweetness and affectionateness of temper that she lived in an ideal world of happiness, the very sight of which made others happy.'[48]

The experience of prolonged grief had a deep spiritual effect. First, he accepted it as an act of divine providence to which he resigned himself, as he did when he failed to take honors in the schools. Second, he experienced a heightened sense of the transitoriness of the world, a frequent subject in his later sermons. 'The days and months fly past me,' he had written on his twenty-third birthday in 1824, 'and I seem as if I would cling hold of them, and hinder them from escaping. There they lie, entombed in the grave of Time, buried with faults and failings and deeds of all sorts, never to appear till the sounding of the last Trump.' Now this sense came home to him again, not only with the death of Mary, but with that of his first spiritual guide, Mr Mayer, who died shortly afterwards. 'This world is but a shadow and a dream,' he assured the widow of his friend. 'We think we see things and we see them not—they do not exist, they die on all sides, things dearest and pleasantest and most beloved. But in heaven we shall all meet and it will be *no* dream.'[49]

Perhaps most important of all was Newman's intense grasp of the reality and presence of another world, an invisible one, existing now, separated from the visible world by a veil but still real, in which Mary dwells. Six months after her death, writing to his sister Jemina, he tells how when riding with companions in the countryside, 'I never felt so intensely the transistory nature of this world as when most delighted with these country scenes. . . . Dear Mary seems embodied in every tree and hid behind every hill. What a veil and curtain this world of sense is! beautifull but still a veil.' Nature from now on speaks of this invisible world behind it, in which Mary dwells and with whom he can communicate. Speaking of a morning solitary ride in the country, he writes Harriett, the eldest of his sisters, the following November, 'A solemn voice seems to chant from every thing. I know whose voice it is—it is her dear voice.'[50] This invisible world in which she dwells will one day become the future world of glory of all the saints, as he writes in one of his several poems about her. These experiences of the invisible world, of which he will become reflectively conscious in reading the Alexandrian Fathers of the Church, is the source of those many sermons on the invisible world in the *Plain and Parochial Sermons.*

The illness and bereavement had the further effect of detaching him from worldly ambitions and setting him back on the road to perfection. He later confessed to Keble that God 'repeatedly and variously chastised me and at last to wean me from the world, He took from me a dear sister—and just at the same time He gave me kind friends to teach me His ways more perfectly.'[51] The new friends were Hurrell Froude, and John Keble himself, the latter of whom he got to know better in the summer of 1828, thanks to the former. From this time on Newman set himself against rising in the Church. All worldly ambition was effectively obliterated, and intellectual pursuits subordinated to the pursuit of holiness. At this time he composed many prayers which are still extant.

Vicar of St Mary's

On 31 January 1828 Hawkins was elected Provost of Oriel, and Newman succeeded him as Vicar of St Mary's on 14 March. It was the beginning of a new stage in his life. Summarizing in the *Apologia* the change that took place in him from 1826 to 1828, he states that up to 1826, 'to no one in Oxford . . . did I open my heart fully and familiarly,' but this changed when he became tutor, composed some well-received essays, preached his first University Sermon, became in 1827 a Public Examiner in the Schools for the B.A. degree, and Vicar of St Mary's in 1828. 'It was to me like the feeling of spring weather after winter; and, if I may so speak, I came out of my shell; I remained out of it till 1841.'[52] Newman had a natural empathy, an ability to enter into the ideas and feelings of others. As a result, once he opened himself to others he had a magnetic attraction which drew more and more people to him, many of whom became close friends. This natural empathy was in time spiritualized and super-naturalized as a result of sufferings, especially mental sufferings, which interiorly he accepted in union with Christ. How much the initial change had to do with his rejection of Evangelicalism he does not say, but it would seem that it did have a connection.

Evangelicals thought it necessary 'to examine the heart with a view to ascertaining whether it is in a spiritual state or no.' Spiritual-mindedness they considered to consist in certain emotions and desires. The system consequently involved 'a continual self-contemplation and reference to self, in all departments of conduct.' In thus striving for a certain frame of mind, there was a reflex action of the mind upon self, which, Newman came to believe, created a subtle, 'an habitual quiet self-esteem,' leading one to prefer one's own views to those of others, and 'a secret, if not avowed persuasion, that he is in a different state from the generality of those around him.'[53] In his journals Newman had recorded that he used to take solitary walks, that he was beset by vain thoughts of his superiority of intellect, and that he looked down upon others. In typical Evangelical fashion he tried to find out if Pusey 'belonged to Christ.' Thus, he reacted condescendingly to him in his initial contacts, and even later quoted from his journals to illustrate his 'high patronizing tone' in referring to him in his journal entries.[54]

Newman was grateful that St Mary's Parish was small enough not to require two sermons on Sunday. Sermons, he thought, should be subordinate to public worship, and parish ministry required more than the performance of the Sunday liturgy. After a year at St Mary's he felt there was not a sufficient private contact with his parishioners which he thought a necessary part of his responsibilities as a pastor, such as visiting the sick and catechizing the children. No child came for Sunday catechizing.[55] One of the reasons for subsequently instituting Saints-Day services in 1830 was, he said, 'because it gives me an opportunity of knowing the more religious part of my Congregation.'[56] Sermons, which he felt people exalted too much in the scale of importance, were no substitute in his eyes for familiar teaching, 'being too short in exposition to embrace the peculiarities of doctrine, and necessarily too general in exhortation to apply to the varieties of character and circumstances of those to whom they are spoken.'[57] Apparently to cope with this intrinsic limitation of a sermon, Newman often applied the theme of a sermon to various types of persons whether sinners or persons in different stages of spiritual development.

Before the end of 1829 Newman began a course of sermons on the liturgy, by which he meant not only the Sunday services but all the rites, ordinances, and sacraments accompanied by suitable prayers which range over the Christian's life from infant baptism to his final departure from earth, as set down in the Book of Common Prayer. One of the effects of these liturgical actions is to help form the Christian character through prayers that express faith, hope, and charity.[58]

The Fathers of the Church

At the beginning of 1829, with the support of fellow tutors Robert Wilberforce and Hurrell Froude, Newman had introduced a modification in the tutorial system which gave them greater contact and influence with their own pupils and obviated the necessity of hiring private tutors. Dornford, the Dean and Senior Tutor, allowed this on a trial basis. Hawkins in due time ordered them to return to the old system, which they refused to do. The Provost stopped assigning Newman pupils, effectively eliminating him from the tutorship. Newman felt that Hawkins did not realize the intensity of his feeling 'that, unless he could make his educational engagements a fulfilment of his ordination vow, he could have no part in them.'[59]

Newman was affected by this change in his life, though he said very little about it. For one thing, what seemed a promising avenue of influence was now closed to him. Second, he had always considered that teaching was his vocation; apparently it was not God's will. Third, there are subtle indications that he was disappointed at his failure to bring about other needed reforms, for example, with the Missionary and Bible Societies. 'All my plans fail. When did I ever succeed in any exertions for others?' Thirty years later Newman remarked on this statement and referred to his sermon, 'Jeremiah, a Lesson for the Disappointed,' preached 12 September 1830, in which he showed how failure led the prophet to a spirit of resignation to God's will.[60] It was not the last time Newman was to face opposition, misunderstanding of his motives and exertions, and apparent failure. He later came to see in his removal from the tutorship the hand of God's providence, insofar as he was now free to take up the study of the Fathers of the Church in depth, having begun to read them chronologically in the summer of 1828, and to compose his first book, the *Arians of the Fourth Century*. The Oxford Movement, he said, humanly speaking, 'never would have been, had he not been deprived of his Tutorship.'[61]

In March 1831 Hugh Rose asked him to write a history of the Council of Nicaea. Newman began work in June but read himself back to the Ante-Nicene history of the Church in which he encountered the Alexandrian Fathers who had a marked influence on his thought and spirituality. Two aspects of their teaching found a resonance in his own thinking: the sacramental view of the universe and the doctrine of the 'economies.' He now came to regard the visible world as subordinate to the invisible world so that events which seem to be complete in themselves actually subserve the invisible world of God's providence. Newman had already been exploring this notion of providence in his sermons on Jewish history. In relation to his own spiritual life it meant that 'one sees Christ revealed to one's soul amid the ordinary actions of the day, as by a sort of sacrament.'[62]

Briefly stated, the doctrine of economy meant that God had adapted Himself to the moral and spiritual conditions of man in various stages of history, thereby preparing him for the fuller revelation in Christ. The practice of the 'Disciplina Arcani' (the discipline of the secret) was an application of the same principle, whereby the Christian teacher only gradually initiated the catechumen into the mysteries of faith. This principle henceforth became fundamental in Newman's thought. He applied it to the use of language to express Truth, particularly Christian mysteries. It gave rise to the Tractarian practice of 'reserve.' He applied it to the harmonization of the different functions of the Church in the preface to the third edition of the *Via Media*. His enemies accused him of having 'economized' as an Anglican, that is, while outwardly professing Anglicanism, he secretly intended to lead men to Rome.[63]

On the other hand, Newman contrasted the Alexandrian Fathers' reverence for revelation with the logical disputatiousness of the Aristotelian schools of Antioch, conducted by the Sophists. Arius was trained in the techniques which, Newman said, were more suited to detect error than to establish truth. Moreover, the continued employment of reason on secular objects generated a spirit of intellectual questioning which, when employed on objects that transcend reason, namely, the truths of revelation, led to heresy. Here was a parallel with the liberalizing spirit of the Oriel noetics who, as Mark Pattison said in his *Memoirs,* called everything into question, appealing to first principles and disallowing authority as a judge in intellectual matters. Newman would be forced to clarify what was and what was not 'rationalism' in dealing with religious truth. This he did in Tract 73, 'On the Introduction of Rationalistic Principles into Religion.'[64]

For some time Newman had become more and more concerned about the state of the Church, its divisions, and the attempt to remove the Creed from the liturgy. 'We live in a novel age. . . . Men hitherto depended on others, and especially the clergy, for religious truth, now each man attempts to judge for himself. . . . All parties seem to acknowledge that the stream of opinion is setting against the Church.' He began to feel that by theological investigation he could make a contribution to Oxford, which, he said, was sadly deficient in it, and that it would be 'his duty to stay.' In an ordination sermon he proclaimed that the Church from its earliest days had always opposed error and sought 'to promote Truth and Holiness.' It was the special duty of a minister in the Church to have 'a systematic view of truth' and to hold theologically correct views, so as to guide others.[65]

Illness in Sicily

Exhausted after completing his book on the *Arians,* Newman accepted an invitation from Hurrell Froude and his father to undertake a Mediterranean journey. After several months journeying, Newman left the Froudes in Rome and decided to return to Sicily alone. At Leonforte he fell deathly ill of a fever, and underwent the third and perhaps the most intense of the three major spiritual experiences associated with an illness. He thought he had been given over to the devil. The first day lying in bed, he felt God was fighting against him, and that at last he knew why, because of self-will. Yet he kept saying to himself, 'I have not sinned against light.' He thought he had shown self-will in returning to Sicily, as well as in the matter of the tutorship. He repented and resolved to do penance by not preaching at St Mary's or anywhere for a length of time 'as a penitent unworthy to show himself.' He recalled that his last act before leaving Oxford was to preach a University sermon on the character of Saul against self-will, so that he seemed to have been predicting his own condemnation. He examined himself, to see whether he had any feelings of resentment against the Provost and therefore had unworthily taken the Holy Sacrament. Yet he kept consoling himself by saying that he had not sinned against light.

Newman then thought he 'would try to obey God's will as far as I could, and, with a dreamy confused notion, which the fever (I suppose) occasioned, thought that in setting off the fourth day from Leonforte, I was *walking* as long as I could in the way of God's commandments, and putting myself in the way of His mercy, as if He would meet me. (Is. xxvi, 8).'[66] After walking seven miles he collapsed and was put up at Castro Giovanni. Cured and on his way back to England, having repented of self-will and resolved to conform his will to God's in loving surrender, he was convinced that he was entering on a new phase of his spiritual journey. So he expressed this in the famous lines of 'Lead Kindly Light,' written when his ship was becalmed in the Straits of Bonifacio, and he was impatient to get home to England.

I was not ever thus, nor prayed that Thou shouldest lead me on.
I loved to chose and see my path; but now Lead Thou me on.

I loved the garish day, and spite of fears, Pride ruled my will;
remember not past years.

Fearful of self-will thereafter, Newman constantly sought approval of
Hurrell Froude with regard to his writings. After Froude's death he
turned more and more to Keble for advice. When Newman was troubled
by the reaction of his bishop to the Tracts and by the objection of Keble's
brother and others to the publication of an English translation of the
Roman Breviary, Keble put this down to sensitiveness, but Newman's
sensitiveness was rather toward God and whether he was not following his
own will. He makes it clear that he was willing to do anything they
would determine.[67]

Later in Oxford Newman began to see the Sicilian experience as a
decisive and providential event in his life, which explains his successive
efforts, starting with the first attempt, 31 August 1834, and ending 25
March 1840, to construct an accurate narrative of all the details of it. Like
the second spiritual experience connected with an illness, this one involved a deepening of the commitment of the first, whose characteristic
principles can be summed up as a commitment to holiness, that is, to
discover the will of God, to be faithful to the light or call given him, by
energetic action, with detachment from worldly aims and ambitions, and
with complete trust in God's providence over his life. It is the unbroken
fidelity to the divine light given him amidst trials, hardships, and misunderstandings that accounts for the consistency of his life, even when he
shed opinions which he came to believe were not true.

The Promotion of Truth and Holiness

Convinced that God had a work for him to do in England, Newman
arrived back in Oxford to be caught up in the beginnings of the Oxford
Movement of which he soon became the acknowledged leader. The Whig
Government, which had produced the Reform Bill of 1832, suppressed
ten Irish episcopal sees. Where would they stop? The Government
seemed to ignore the rights of the Church, and in its reforming mood
might go on to change the liturgy, or even to disestablish the Church
altogether. Newman, in a campaign to rouse the nation, began a series of

tracts. In the first one he issued a rallying cry to choose sides. The Church has an intrinsic authority, independent of the state, based upon the bishops as successors of the apostles and, therefore, with internal powers and spiritual resources.

What Newman dreaded was a liberalizing tendency which, if it once got a foothold in the Church, might destroy it. By 'liberalism' Newman meant doctrinal liberalism, the belief that dogma is but opinion, that one religion is as good as another, as long as it is sincerely held.[68] It was sensible therefore to enlarge the Church of England by purging its liturgy of creeds, thus allowing all Protestants to join under a broad umbrella united by a moral rather than a credal bond. This tendency to equate dogma with theological opinion was manifested in the lectures delivered in 1832 at Oxford by Dr R. D. Hampden, who was subsequently appointed Regius Professor of Divinity. In opposing Hampden Newman was careful not to attack him personally but merely his ideas as set forth in his writings. As a controversialist he presented his opponent's position with clarity and force, so much so that some complained he conceded too much. These principles flowed from his realization of the demands of charity and justice.

Newman's campaign against Liberalism made significant gains, and although he made gestures toward the Evangelicals, they came into open conflict with him, accusing him of Romanizing the Church.[69] In the *Apologia* Newman affirmed without giving any explanation that the Evangelicals played into the hands of the Liberals. This was the reason: Whatever they held in theory, in practice they were less strict in their standards of orthodoxy. The 'admission of (what they call) the strict and technical niceties of doctrine, whether about the Consubstantiality of the Son or the Hypostatic Union, is scarcely part of the definition of a spiritual believer. And hence there is a disproportionate attention paid to the doctrines connected with the work of Christ, in comparison of those which relate to His Person.'[70] William Wilberforce was a typical example. In his book, *A Practical View of Christianity*, he wrote, 'I think Niceties and Subtleties are the ruin of religion.' And one of his biographers comments that he was introducing 'a new sphere of tolerance among men of conflicting opinions and equal sincerity.'[71]

It was to the old Anglican High Church tradition therefore that Newman turned for support. This was the tradition which had come down from Laud and Andrewes, Charles I, Pearson, Bull, and the non-Jurors. To some, such as Keble, the doctrines proposed were those he had learned from his own clergyman father, but to the ordinary common-sense Englishman it seemed like a return to popery. As time went on and the threat of Government intervention receded, it was imperative to show how Tractarianism stood in relation to Rome as well as in relation to dissenters and to the Evangelicals in the Church of England, whom Newman referred to as extreme Protestants or simply Protestants. This he attempted to do in the tracts called *Via Media* (Tracts 38 and 41) and later in greater detail in *Lectures on the Prophetical Office of the Church* (now vol. 1 of *Via Media*). Newman proposed, as the path for the English Church to walk, a middle way between what he called the extremes of Romanism, which he said had corrupted the original revelation by additions, and Protestantism. The latter emphasized the invisible Church of the convert-ed and ignored the Catholic aspects of the one, holy, catholic and apos-tolic Church of the Apostles' Creed, particularly the visible Church with its sacraments, the conduits of grace and the mediating instruments of Christ's redemption to its members. This Catholic tradition the Re-formers had not entirely erased. It was embedded in the Book of Common Prayer and in the Thirty-Nine Articles.

This Catholic tradition Newman also found preserved in the Anglican divines of the seventeenth century, who had looked to the Fathers of the Church for purity of doctrine. Antiquity, therefore, becomes the test of genuine doctrine. On the one hand, Newman had to present a connected series of writings from the Anglican divines on certain Catholic doctrines, such as apostolic succession and the doctrine of baptismal regeneration (denied by the Evangelicals), which he did in Tracts 74 and 76, and the doctrine of the Eucharistic sacrifice, which Pusey did in Tract 81. On the other hand, Pusey, with the help of Newman and Keble as editors, published translations of the Fathers of the Church. As Newman later said, these were the authorities. One had only to read them to become aware and convinced of what was primitive and Catholic truth.

The Parochial Sermons

The Oxford Movement, however, was something more than an eccle-siastical and ecclesiological battle. R. W. Church wrote in *The Oxford*

Movement (1893): 'The movement, whatever else it was, or whatever else it became, was in its first stages a movement for deeper religion, for a more real and earnest self-discipline, for a loftier morality, for more genuine self-devotion to serious life, than had ever been seen in Oxford.'[72]

Of the various means of renewing the spiritual life of the Church, it was widely admitted that the most effective were Newman's preaching and the publication of his *Parochial Sermons*.[73] The power of the sermons stemmed from Newman's own personal and deep meditations on Christian realities, but no doubt the spiritual need for them played a role as well, for the standard of preaching at the time was, in general, at a low ebb. High churchmen were for the most part dry, while Evangelical sermons had become stylized and boring. The latter concentrated on the beginnings of the spiritual life, the need for forgiveness, and the assurance of such. They had little to say about building up the spiritual life or the details of growth in obedience and in Christian living. As Newman told Samuel Wilberforce, an Evangelical, 'All the sermons are the same' and they 'can never say a thing in a natural way—they are always casting an eye on their system.'

If, at times, Newman's sermons seem stern and demanding, Newman meant them to be that way. In the same letter to Wilberforce, who criticized Newman's first volume of sermons for not talking of the influence of the Holy Spirit, a favorite topic of Evangelical preachers, Newman remarked: 'My Sermons are on subjects connected with sanctification. My reason for dwelling on the latter subject was my conviction *that we require the Law* not the Gospel in this age—we want rousing—we want the claims of duty and the details of obedience set before us strongly—and that is what has led me to enlarge on our part of the work *not on the Spirit's*.'[74] In subsequent volumes, however, Newman did preach on the indwelling of the Holy Spirit.

Newman's purpose in the sermons he preached at St Mary's was to lead men and women to realize vividly for themselves the mysteries of faith and to comprehend authentic Christianity as a concrete way of life, not merely as an abstract program for living. Evangelical preachers' repetition of certain phrases and formulas of their system leads, he said, to 'unreal words' and unreal professions, not to embracing the realities for which these words stand. To create contact with these realities Newman had to reveal to his audience the hidden deceptions and secret maneuvers people use to escape from truth and themselves. He confronted them with their subtle self-deceptions, unrecognized pretensions, and spiritual insincerities, to lead them to self-knowledge and an unconditional willingness to be transformed by Christ. By an accumulation of biblical examples, suggestions, and analyses of attitudes of mind, Newman gradually brought his hearers to assimilate the meaning of Christian truths in relation to their lives. Finally, Newman's achievement in these sermons lay in the profoundly difficult task of making the invisible world, so real to him, real for his hearers as well. In this he was, according to testimonies of the time, entirely successful.

Undoubtedly Newman preached a stricter religion than that which obtained among clergy and laity alike, and he opposed the comfortable worldliness into which the Church was said to have fallen. In his sketches of the Fathers of the Church he wrote approvingly of the ascetical practices of the monks and Fathers, whether celibacy, fasting, or penances. The Evangelicals looked upon these practices as 'Romanish' and therefore thought they should have no place in a reformed Church. Writers have characterized Newman and his fellow Tractarians as serious and 'earnest,' and it is true these qualities radiate from his sermons, but so were the Evangelicals thus characterized, and Newman warned his listeners against *their* 'earnestness.' The essence of faith, on which they placed so great an emphasis is not, he said, in having right feelings. Impetuous feelings may be the first step in religion, for example, repentance for sin, but they wear away. Feelings come and go. The highest Christian temper is peace and tranquility, not sentiment and tumultuous feeling.[75]

The Evangelicals, rejecting baptismal regeneration, had constant recourse to the Lutheran doctrine of 'justification by faith alone.' But what does this mean in the concrete? asked Newman. 'I want a real doctrine, containing an intelligible, tangible, practical view which one can take and use.' This he masterfully presented in his 'Lectures on Justification'; it is a work which appeals both to man's abstract intelligence and to his devotional nature. As Bremond remarked, he 'treats doctrine not as abstract theory, but as the expression of a living reality in which the Christian soul finds its spiritual sustenance.' That reality is Christ. 'True faith,' Newman wrote, 'is what may be called colourless, like air or water; it is but the medium through which the soul sees Christ, and the soul as little rests upon it or contemplates it, as the eye can see the air.'[76]

Coldness in devotion, a criticism levelled against the High and Dry party in the Church, Newman sought to remedy by introducing long-forgotten Anglican devotional works such as *Sacra Privata. The Private Meditations, Devotions, and Prayers of the Rev. T. Wilson,* Oxford 1840, and *The Devotions of Bishop Andrewes,* translated from the Greek and arranged anew, Oxford 1842. His own personal prayers were organized along the lines of Bishop Andrewes. 'The forms in which the prayers are couched, their orderly arrangement, their tone at once restrained and reverential, their economic phraseology, all commended them to him as models to be adopted and followed,' wrote Henry Tristram.[77] Newman also republished Christopher Sutton's *Disce Vivere. Learn to live* and *Godly Meditations upon the most holy Sacrament of the Lord's Supper,* and Anthony Sparrow's *A Rationale upon the Book of Common Prayer of the Church of England.*

Lead Thou Me On

In 1839, when he experienced his first doubts about the Anglican Church, Newman noted in his diary details of increased strictness in his customary private fasting and concluded with the words, '*Gratias tibi Domine*—whither are thou leading me?' He preached his sermon, 'Divine Calls' which ended on the note that nothing could be compared with this one aim, 'of not being disobedient to a heavenly vision.'[78] Prudently he revealed his doubts only to Henry Wilberforce and Frederic Rogers, two intimate friends, and later to Robert Wilberforce when he felt obliged in conscience to do so. Although he had no intention at this time of becoming a Catholic, he outlined in a letter what he thought the proper course to be followed by one faced with the growing conviction that it was a duty to become a Catholic, as a number of younger members of the movement were beginning to feel.

> . . . did I see cause to suspect that the Roman Church was in the right, I would try not to be unfaithful to the light given to me. And if any future time, I have any view opened to me, I will try not to turn from it, but will pursue it, wherever it may lead. I am not aware of having any hindrance, whether from fear of clamour, or regard for consistency, or even love of friends, which could keep me from joining the Church of Rome, were I persuaded I ought to do so. . . .

He went on to say that such a step should not be taken without a two- or three-year period of deliberation, accompanied by spiritual exercises, and without seeking the guidance of others.[79] This pretty much summarizes Newman's program after 1841 when he retired from the movement to Littlemore to live a semi-monastic life of prayer, fasting, and study. With extraordinary prudence he advanced step by step. He retracted statements against Rome, and then, since Keble acquiesced that there would be nothing wrong in his resigning from St Mary's, he did so, fulfilling the resolution he adopted, *'Do* what your present state of opinion requires in the light of duty, and let the *doing* tell; speak by *acts.'*[80] On 24 September 1843 he preached his last sermon in St Mary's and at Littlemore the following day he concluded his last sermon in the Anglican Church with the plea for prayers 'that in all things he may know God's will, and at all times he may be ready to fulfil it.'[81]

His mental suffering during the following two years was intense, especially the pain he was causing others and the fear that if he made a wrong step, he would lead those who would follow him either into error or into skepticism. His greatest fear was that he was suffering from a delusion because of some secret past fault, and as a result had become 'judicially blind.' Revealing to Keble all the instances of God's personal providence over him, starting with his first conversion, up to the graces given him in recent years to live a stricter life, he asked, 'Has He led me thus far to destroy me in the wilderness?' His trust in God, however, was unshaken. 'The great remedy of all uneasiness is to feel that we are in God's hands, and to entertain an earnest desire to do His will.'[82]

Though there were many slanders, misrepresentations, and misunderstandings of his motives and actions that could have caused him to act from resentment, he was determined to go by reason, not by feeling, and when he was not only convinced that the Catholic Church was the one true Church of Christ but also that he had an obligation in conscience to enter it, he did so promptly, on 9 October 1845.[83]

The Path of St Philip Neri

Newman's conversion was admittedly a heroic act. He was ostracized by family, friends, and society. This was a great sacrifice, the greatest, he later admitted, that he had to make in becoming a Catholic and one that he had continually to offer up. He was sustained in it by the presence of

Christ in the Blessed Sacrament, and this devotion became the central and fundamental one of his subsequent life as a Catholic.[84] Dr Wiseman and Dominic Barbieri were equally impressed by Newman's docility.[85] He came to learn and to submit. He was unfortunately catechized like a child by an Italian priest, probably Fr Acqueroni, whom Wiseman appointed chaplain to the group living at Maryvale.[86] He also attempted to adopt certain devotional practices which were rudely thrust upon him but which were not suited to his temperament or habitual devotional life, such as 'the prayers necessary for gaining certain indulgences.' He also had 'a particular dread of making resolutions.' On the other hand, the mass, visits to the Blessed Sacrament, the rosary, litanies, the breviary— all these gave him pleasure.[87]

In his retreat before taking minor orders Newman records that he long prayed that he might never be rich, but found it hard to say 'Let me be poor.' Newman's view toward poverty was the same as an Anglican and as a Catholic. On the one hand he believed that 'poverty is better than riches.' On the other hand, he did not pray for it or other sufferings, but only that he be able to bear them well if God brought them upon him. (*AW*, pp. 236, 238, 246; *MD*, p. 348) He gave generously in alms, loved the poor, and at various times in his life he was in need of money. He always lived in great simplicity, even as a cardinal.[88]

From 8 to 17 April Newman made a retreat at St Eusebio in Rome in preparation for his ordination to the priesthood. He has left a searching psychological self-analysis, in which he tries to explain in multifaceted detail the reasons why he seemed unable to rise to higher perfection. Père Louis Bouyer, who in the original French edition of his life of Newman was the first to publish this document, commented on it: 'Only to the saints is it granted thus to bring the detecting ray to bear on all their soul's distress, all their sins and failings; but the very fact that they behold them so clearly is a sign that they have already got the better of them.'

With equal truthfulness Newman nevertheless acknowledges certain habitual aspects of his spiritual life:

1) he has no desire for wealth, power, or a great name;
2) if God so ordained, he would give up health and 'a certain measure of comfort' which he likes;
3) he habitually refers all things to God;

4) he has retained faith and trust in God and in the efficacy of prayer, if not so lively as it once was;

5) he has retained a certain cheerfulness and gentleness notwithstanding that the former is not what it once was;

6) he has a habitual inward sense of the Divine Presence everywhere, a good conscience, and the peace of mind that flows from it.[89]

When Newman was ordained in the Church of England, he recorded in his journal, 'I have the responsibility of souls on me to the day of my death.' Now prior to his ordination in the Catholic Church he seems to have been similarly affected: 'the responsibilities of orders grow greater and greater upon me, as I approach them.'[90] After a good deal of prayer and having examined various religious congregations, Newman and his companions chose the Oratorian way of life. An Oratorian congregation is a small group of secular priests, rarely more than thirteen at the most, living in common a religious life, the bond of union being not vows but charity. Newman returned to England with a papal brief to set up the Oratory in Birmingham and elsewhere. In granting the brief the Pope added a special mission which Newman had not petitioned for, namely, 'and among those in the higher ranks, the more learned, and generally among the more educated.' Certain adaptations were made from the original rule of St Philip, for example, that they could engage in certain educational activities.[91]

St Philip Neri thereafter became Newman's great patron and a model for imitation. There are constant references to him in Newman's letters, and in a tribute to him at the end of the 'Discourses on University Education,' he said Philip wanted to be 'an ordinary individual priest as others: and his weapons should be but unaffected humility and unpretending love. All he did was to be done by the light, and fervour, and convincing eloquence of his personal character and his easy conversation.'[92] This could have been written as an epitome of Newman's own life as a Catholic.

There was one more spiritual disposition of which Philip was his model. In his private journal, when all his efforts for the Church had been frustrated, he confided:

It has become my *lifelong* prayer, and Thou hast granted it, that I should be set aside in this world. Now then let me make it once again. O Lord, bless what I write and prosper it—let it do much good, let it have much success; but let no praise come to me on that account in my lifetime. Let me go on living, let me die, as I have hitherto lived. Long before I knew St Philip I wished '*nesciri*'. Let me more and more learn from Thy grace '*sperni*', and '*spernere me sperni*'.

At the same time he prayed that no contempt that came upon him would injure the future of the Oratory.[93]

And so when he was misrepresented at Rome, he endured it in the spirit of St Philip, to which he added the example of St Alphonsus and St Calasanctius.[94] Also one of his main apostolates was to remain hidden until long after his death. It was handling an ever-increasing correspondence, much of which was concerned with helping persons of all religious persuasions with their religious and spiritual difficulties. During the 1860s he once wrote twenty letters in one day, eighteen in another. In his letters of sympathy he often repeated what he said in letters as an Anglican—that sufferings and trials are a sign of God's special love—and this was his habitual conviction. Richard Simpson summed up what many felt and indeed expressed in letters to Newman: 'The charity you show to men in difficulties is boundless, and you will like to know is often most efficacious.'[95]

Newman's greatest trial as a Catholic was to be misunderstood and unappreciated by ecclesiastical superiors. In his private journal he noted that although he worked for God's glory, still there was a natural desire to please superiors.[96] Subsequent entries in the journal reveal that he underwent an interior purification of his motives which resulted in an interior tranquility and peace.

Personal Charism

Just as when he was an Anglican Newman felt a special call, so did he become conscious of a special vocation in the Catholic Church. It was to educate the Catholic mind and to raise the intellectual level of the Church in England so as to meet the challenge of religious liberalism and 'infidelity' which he prophetically foresaw and characterized in 'A Form of Infidelity of the Day.'[97] He responded to this call with efforts on behalf of the laity as Rector of the Catholic University, in his support of the conductors of the *Rambler* magazine, and in his defense of freedom in the Church in the latter part of the *Apologia,* to name but a few. These brought him into conflict with the Ultramontanes, who were successful in curbing his activities and bringing on him intense interior suffering.

In fulfillment of part of this special vocation, he composed the *Grammar of Assent,* for which he had prepared himself by reading, investigation, and writing for over twenty years. While he felt it his duty to submit to the prescriptions of the Church, whatever his own personal judgment, the Church did not always speak with equal binding authority. When Ullathorne his bishop condemned the writings of Richard Simpson and the *Rambler,* he promptly submitted his canonical obedience. Later when he read Simpson, he thought Ullathorne had misrepresented Simpson, and so he wrote Ullathorne saying that his obedience did not involve his judgment. W. G. Ward, Newman's most outspoken opponent, admired Newman's honesty and bravery in risking Ullathorne's friendship in behalf of truth.[98]

Newman was not disturbed by difference of opinion in the Church. 'God means such differences to be an exercise of charity,' he told Ward. What he did object to was the lack of a public forum such as the different theological schools once provided for debating these issues. Consequently, at a time when the Church was retreating into a fortress mentality he stood as a beacon for those who looked for a more open Church. Unafraid of the discoveries of Darwin or of other scientists and of biblical studies, he advocated freedom of research with the quiet confidence that there could ultimately be no conflict between the findings of history and science and the truths of revelation. His handling of the question of freedom and authority in the Church as well as his attitude toward science and the modern world were echoed in the decrees of the Second Vatican Council.

So too in his relations with non-Catholics Newman displayed remarkable understanding and good will. Distressed at what to Catholics seemed like Pusey's attack on Catholic devotion to Our Lady in his supposed *Eirenicon,* he remarked to Keble that 'the first duty of charity is to try and enter into the mind and feelings of others.' Newman's reply in his *Letter to Pusey* is a model of true ecumenical dialogue. What Pusey later said of Newman's bigletto speech when he was made a Cardinal can be applied to this *Letter:* 'quite like the old John Henry Newman speaking out the truth, yet not wounding a single heart.'[99]

Continuity and Development

Newman's vision and practice of the Christian life as a Catholic was a continuation of his understanding and practice of it in the Church of England.[100] 'What in the concrete circumstances is God's will for me?' Or put another way, 'Where is God's providence leading me?' Hence his constant recourse to prayer for light and guidance. He never undertook a work of consequence without having made it the subject of previous prayers including masses, litanies, and novenas. Consequently, he was able, according to Fr William Neville, his literary executor, to accept many trials and setbacks with remarkable equanimity, because whatever turned out he took as God's answer to his prayers. And there were many set-backs indeed.

Newman also believed that God ordinarily reveals His will through the wishes of superiors. There was no work, even if it went against his own will and judgment, that he would not undertake if he were asked by superiors. At the request of Wiseman he received Faber and his followers as Oratorians, though their spirit was different. He accepted the rectorship of the Catholic University in Dublin because the Holy Father wanted a Catholic University. He began the Oratory School in order to fulfill the special mission the Holy Father had given in the brief to set up the Oratory. Before accepting the editorship of the *Rambler* magazine he tried to ascertain God's will, and he took upon himself the editorship though it was contrary to his own will. When asked by his bishop to resign as editor after one issue, he did so promptly. On the occasion of his being prevented from starting the Mission at Oxford, he wrote, 'It has been God's Blessed Will that I should have been stopped.' Asked a second time by his bishop to take on the mission at Oxford, he agreed to do so lest he be deaf to a divine call, but he was prepared to give it up if this was decided by superiors or otherwise indicated that it was not a call. He undertook the task of translating the Bible when this was decreed by a synod.

Newman's writing as a Catholic has to be situated in the context of his Oratorian vocation. Writing had a long tradition in the history of the Oratory, but Newman was an occasional writer. Writing was not the most prominent part of his life as a Catholic, which was taken up with the ordinary and daily tasks of the Oratory: saying mass, hearing confessions, visiting the sick, dusting the books in the library, writing reports to the parents of students at the Oratory School, training the students to act in Latin plays, and helping out the poor in the parish.

Most of Newman's publications were in response to a call, starting with the *Lectures on Difficulties of Anglicans.* The *Idea of a University* and his other educational writings were prompted by his position as first rector of a nascent university. *Lectures on the Present Position of Catholics in England* arose from the so-called papal aggression at the time of the restoration of the hierarchy in England. The *Apologia* and the *Letter to Pusey* were responses to a call to defend the clergy and Catholic devotion to Mary respectively. When requested by several bishops not to write on papal infallibility at the time of the First Vatican Council he complied. Later, though requested to write on the Council, he refrained because he did not feel called to it. When that call came on the occasion of Gladstone's attack on the Vatican decrees, though pressure was put upon him not to, he wrote the *Letter to the Duke of Norfolk* in accordance with the dictate of his conscience. In all his writings Newman had the habitual intention of submitting them to the judgment of the Church.

There was little that Newman in becoming a Catholic had to give up and little that he had to add to his understanding of the Christian way of life. His presentation of the message of sin and redemption hardly differs from that he had presented as an Anglican. The style and rhetoric, so much more florid than that in the *Parochial and Plain Sermons,* as well as the greater length of each discourse, have kept the *Discourses to Mixed Congregations* from exercising the same enduring appeal. It may be that the Italian missionary style of preaching in England prompted him to adopt a more flamboyant style, though no satisfactory explanation has been given for the change. When he came to publish the *Sermons on Various Occasions* in 1857 he was no longer anxious to conform to what he thought or was told was expected of him. In them he reverted to his old plain style. The first eight were preached before the Catholic University of Ireland in 1856 and 1857, and contain some of his finest sermons, including, 'Intellect the Instrument of Religious Training,' 'Omnipotence in Bonds,' and the two sermons on St Paul.

As has been said, there is a continuity between Newman's vision of the spiritual life as an Anglican and as a Catholic. Insofar as he put the vision into practice his actions as a Catholic were simply the application of the same principles to different circumstances in his life.

The widening and deepening of Newman's vision of the Christian revelation may be summed up in an ecumenical letter he wrote a few years before his death:

I will not close our correspondence without testifying my simple love and adhesion to the Catholic Roman Church, . . . and did I wish to give a reason for this full and absolute devotion, what should, what can, I say, but that those great and burning truths, which I learned when a boy from evangelical teaching, I have found impressed upon my heart with fresh and ever increasing force by the Holy Roman Church? That Church has added to the simple evangelicalism of my first teachers, but it has obscured, diluted, enfeebled, nothing of it—on the contrary, I have found a power, a resource, a comfort, a consolation in our Lord's divinity and atonement, in His Real Presence, in communion in His Divine and Human Person, which all good Catholics indeed have, but which Evangelical Christians have but faintly.[101]

Notes

1. *KC*, pp. 115, 393–94.
2. *LD* I, 251.
3. *GA*, pp. 113–15.
4. *KC*, pp. 317–18.
5. *AW*, p. 250.
6. *MD*, p. 307.
7. *VRS*, p. 12.
8. *LD* XVII, 232.
9. *PPS* I, 18, pp. 228ff.; *OS*, 1, pp. 10–11.
10. *VRS*, pp. 15, 17–19.
11. *AW*, p. 268.
12. *AW*, p. 172.
13. *AW*, p. 150.
14. *AW*, p. 250.
15. *AW*, pp. 165, 268.
16. 17 November 1817, BOA: A.10.4.
17. *Apo.*, p. 5.
18. *Apo.*, p. 49.
19. *Dev.*, pp. 346–52. See Richard M. Liddy, 'Spirituality and the Dogmatic Principle,' *The Priest*, 43 (June 1987), 41–45.

20. *Apo.*, p. 4. Writing to Miss Giberne he quoted this as example of 'catachresis' or montsrous metaphor, e.g., 'darkness visible.' The context of the sermon in which he explains it makes clear that it does not isolate one from relatives and friends. See *PPS*, I, 2, pp. 18–21, *LD* XXVII, 359. See also *PPS*, V, 19, pp. 279–80.

21. *Apo.*, p. 7.

22. *Apo.* p. 7.

23. Louis Bouyer, *Newman: His Life and Spirituality*, London 1958, p. 28.

24. William Beveridge, *Private Thoughts Upon Religion* and *Private Thoughts upon a Christian Life*. See *LD* I, 32–34.

25. J.H.N. 14 Oct. 1874. *LD* I, 30, n. 1.

26. *KC*, p. 117.

27. *AW*, p. 149.

28. *AW*, pp. 159–60; *LD* I, 87–99.

29. 'A Collection of Scripture passages setting forth in due order of succession the doctrines of Christianity.' (BOA, A.9.1). See Thomas Sheridan, *Newman on Justification*, New York 1967, pp. 50–57; *AW*, pp. 161, 166–67, 172.

30. *AW*, pp. 174ff., 178, 188–89, 194, 196, 198.

31. *AW*, p. 189; Bouyer, p. 28.

32. *AW*, pp. 165–66.

33. *AW*, p. 175.

34. *AW*, p. 194.

35. *AW*, pp. 176, 179.

36. *AW*, p. 201.

37. *AW*, pp. 77, 79.

38. *AW*, pp. 78, 202, 204.

39. *AW*, p. 78; *Apo.*, pp. 9–10.

40. *PPS* II, 15, pp. 169–70.

41. See sermons on sin and justification in *John Henry Newman. Sermons 1824–1843*, vol. 2, edited by Vincent Ferrer Blehl, S.J., Oxford 1993.

42. *PPS* I, p. 6.

43. For example, 'The Spiritual Mind,' *PPS* I, sermon 6; 'Profession without Practice,' *PPS* I, sermon 10; 'Ventures of Faith,' *PPS* IV, 20, pp. 301ff.; *PPS* V, 16, p. 226.

44. William Wilberforce, *A Practical View of the Prevailing System of Professed Christians in the higher and middle Classes in this Country, contrasted with real Christianity*, London 1834, pp. 106, 115; William Beveridge, *Private Thoughts upon a Christian Life*, London 1817 in the chapter 'Thoughts upon Christian Education'; William Law, *A Serious Call to a Devout and Holy Life*, London 1906, pp. 10, 18.

45. *AW*, pp. 89–96.

46. *AW*, p. 210.

47. *Apo.*, pp. 13–14.

48. *AW*, pp. 212–13; *LD* II, xiii.

49. *AW*, p. 196; *LD* II, 58.

50. *LD* II, 69–70, 108.

51. *KC*, p. 315.

52. *Apo.*, pp. 15–16.

53. 'Self-Contemplation,' *PPS* II, 15, pp. 163–74.

54. *AW*, pp. 175, 178, 187–88, 190–91 (cf. p. 75).

55. *John Henry Newman Sermons 1824–1843,* vol. 1, ed. Placid Murray, OSB, Oxford 1991, xv, 6, 26, n. 5; *LD* II, 337.

56. *LD* II, 201–2.

57. *Sermons 1824–1843,* I, p. 6. For Newman's view on Catechism and preaching, see *LD* V, 44–48.

58. *Sermons 1824–1843,* I, sermons 8 to 16.

59. *AW*, p. 103.

60. *LD* II, 289, and n. 1. See also 'How difficult it is for such as know they have gifts suitable to the Church's needs to refrain themselves till God makes a way for their use,' (*PPS* III, p. 53).

61. *AW*, p. 96.

62. *Apo.*, pp. 26–28; *Sermons 1824–1843,* II, sermons on Old Testament History; *PPS* VIII, 11, p. 165.

63. *Apo.*, pp. 269–71, and Note F. 'Economy,' pp. 343–47.

64. *Ari.*, pp. 25–38. Mark Pattison, *Memoirs,* London 1885, p. 79; *Ess.* I.

65. *LD* II, 129–30; 367; sermon no. 323, 'On the Ministerial Order, as an existing divine institution. Ordination Sermon.' 18 Dec. 1831.

66. *AW*, pp. 121ff.; *LD* IV, 8.

67. 'I seem to write things to no purpose as wanting your imprimatur,' To H. Froude, 18 Jan. 1835, *LD* V, 9; *LD*, VI, 347–48, 350.

68. *Apo.*, pp. 30–32; 'Liberalism,' Note A, pp. 385ff. For Hampden, see *Apo.*, pp. 57–58.

69. *LD* VI, 9 and nn. 1, 12, 18.

70. *PPS* II, 15, pp. 166–67.

71. John Pollock, *Wilberforce,* New York 1978, p. 153.

72. R. W. Church, *The Oxford Movement,* London 1890, p. 302.

73. Church, p. 130; J. C. Shairp, *Studies in Poetry and Philosophy,* 3d ed., Edinburgh 1876, pp. 247–49.

74. *LD* V, 21–22.

75. 'Religious Emotion,' *PPS* I, sermon 14.

76. Henri Bremond, *The Mystery of Newman*, trans. H. C. Corrance, London 1907, pp. 125ff.; *Jfc.*, pp. 302–3, 336.

77. H. Tristram, 'With Newman at Prayer,' *Newman Centenary Essays*, ed. H. Tristram, London 1945, p. 113.

78. 'Divine Calls,' *PPS* VIII, 2, p. 32.

79. Letter to S. F. Wood, 10 Nov. 1839 to be given to Robert Williams or not as he thought best. BOA (A.PC) not sent.

80. *Apo.*, p. 216.

81. *Moz.* II, p. 424; 'The Parting of Friends,' *SD*, 26, p. 409.

82. *KC*, pp. 314–18. Gordon Huntington Harper, ed., *Cardinal Newman and William Froude: A Correspondence*, Baltimore 1933, pp. 50–51.

83. *Apo.*, pp. 230–31; *KC*, pp. 293, 355, n. 1; *LD* XI, xxviii.

84. *LD* XI, 129; XX, 59–60, 400, 449. 'Loyalty of Cardinal Newman,' The *Month*, 70 (Nov. 1890), 306–7.

85. Wilfrid Ward, *The Life of John Henry Cardinal Newman*, 2 vols., London 1912, I, p. 99. Frederico Dell'Addolarata, C.P., *Il Beato Domenico della Madre di Deo*, Roma 1963, p. 389.

86. Emily Bowles, *Memorials of John Henry Newman, Cardinal Deacon 1881–84*, BOA.

87. *AW*, pp. 246, 255.

88. *AW*, pp. 237–38; *LD* XI, 307.

89. Bouyer, p. 271; *AW*, pp. 239–42.

90. *LD* XII, 15.

91. Placid Murray, OSB, ed., *Newman the Oratorian: His Unpublished Oratory Papers*, Dublin 1969, pp. 423–29, 433.

92. *Idea*, p. 236

93. *AW*, pp. 252–53.

94. *LD* XXIII, 204.

95. *LD* XXVII, 258.

96. *AW*, pp. 251, 262–63ff.

97. *Idea*, pp. 381–91.

98. *LD* XX, 379, n. 2. For Newman's views on freedom and authority in the Church, see my article 'John Henry Newman on Freedom and Authority in the Church,' The *Priest*, 39 (Mar. 1983), 10–15.

99. *LD* XXII, 69; XXIX, 144, n. 1.

100. The following is developed more fully in my paper, 'Newman's Personal Endeavour as a Catholic to follow the "Light" and the "Call,"' *Newman Studien*, Sigmaringendorf 1988, XII, 27–34.

101. *LD*, XXXI, 189.

PART TWO

Newman's Spiritual Theology

I   Turning to God

Chapter One

The Call to Holiness

Conversion

The sincere Christian accepts as a fundamental principle that he has been created by God and that his true happiness consists in serving Him in this life and being conjoined with Him for eternity. To serve God in this life a man must become holy. Moreover, there is a nexus between entering into eternal life and holiness, for 'supposing a man of unholy life were suffered to enter heaven, *he would not be happy there.*' He must first become 'holy as God is holy.' Consequently, a sincere Christian tries to become holy, but he soon realizes that he falls short of what is demanded of him. The more he strives to please God, the more he realizes his failures, and so he is continually turning away from sin and turning to God. (*PPS* I, sermons 1 and 2; VIII, 8, p. 116)

Conversion is often looked upon as a turning from *a life of sin* to God. As already noted, Newman underwent such a conversion experience at age fifteen with the help of Evangelical writers.[1] The Evangelicals wrote of conversion as occurring at a definite time, which is the beginning of a religious life. It was a one-time affair and complete. They described various stages of the experience: 'conviction of sin, terror, despair, news of the free and full salvation, apprehension of Christ, sense of pardon, assurance of salvation, joy and peace, and so on to final perseverance.' Newman was later surprised to realize that he did not pass through these stages. Indeed, after reading the *Apologia* Evangelicals wrote him that he had yet to be converted. (*AW*, pp. 79–80, 172)

When Newman relinquished Evangelicalism, he changed his view of conversion. He affirmed that 'conversion then is a process, not the commencement of a religious course—the gradual changing not an initial change. . . . *Baptism* is God's first time—and no other can be definitely

named. . . . every baptised person is under a process of divine influence
and sanctification, a process often interrupted, often given over, then
resumed, irregularly carried on, heartily entered into, finally completed,
as the case may be.'² Newman therefore warned against looking at conversion as happening at one definite time; rather it is a series of calls by God
given to the individual at various times in his life under the guidance of
God's providence, and to which he responds in faith.³ 'He calls us again
and again . . . to sanctify and glorify us.' (*PPS* III, 7, p. 90; VIII, 5, pp.
225–26; 'Divine Calls,' *PPS* VIII, sermon 2)

What did Newman mean by saying, 'baptism is God's first time'?
Newman came to accept what is called 'baptismal regeneration,' which
was denied generally by the Evangelicals. What he meant was that the
baptized person is reborn. The seeds of holiness are planted within him,
but 'seeds are intended to grow into trees. We are regenerated in order
that we may be renewed daily after the Image of Him who has regenerated us.' 'The new birth of the Holy Spirit sets the soul in motion in a
heavenly way; it gives us good thoughts and desires, enlightens and
purifies us, and prompts us to seek God. In a word . . . it gives a
spiritual *life*; it opens the eyes of the mind, so that we begin to see God in
all things by faith, and hold continual intercourse with Him by prayer;
and if we cherish these gracious influences, we shall become holier and
wiser and more heavenly, year by year, our hearts being ever in a course of
change from darkness to light, from the ways and works of Satan to the
perfection of Divine obedience.' (*PPS* VII, 15, p. 210. See also *PPS* V,
11, pp. 158–59; V, 13, pp. 178–84; V, 24, p. 351).

Newman regarded Christian holiness as the harmonious, complete,
and integrated development of all the powers of nature and grace with
which one is endowed. (*US*, 3, p. 48) This is the ideal; in practice it is
achieved only with struggle and after a long period of time, unless God
produces it quickly in an individual case.

> The perfect Christian state is that in which our duty and our pleasure are
> the same, when what is right and true is natural to us, and in which
> God's 'service is perfect freedom.' And this is the state towards which all
> true Christians are tending . . . an utter and absolute captivity of their
> will to His will, is their fullness and joy and everlasting life. But it is not
> so with the best of us, except in part. Upon our regeneration indeed, we
> have a seed of truth and holiness planted within us . . . but still we have

that old nature to subdue. . . . We have a work, a conflict all through life. We have to master and bring under all we are, all we do, expelling all disorder and insubordination, and teaching and impressing on every part of us, of soul and body, its due place and duty, till we are wholly Christ's in will, affections, and reason, as we are by profession; in St Paul's words '. . . bringing into captivity every thought to the obedience of Christ.' (*PPS* IV, 1, pp. 4–5)

All growth implies change, but the great obstacle to growth in holiness is the unwillingness on our part *to* change. 'We do not like to let go of our old selves.' Moreover, even if we abstractly acknowledge a desire to change, when particular calls are sent to us through conscience, we shrink from them and are content to remain unchanged.[4] Also this is in one way or another 'willfulness, the unaccountable desire of acting short of simple obedience to God's will, a repugnance of unreserved self-surrender and submissiveness to Him.' Yet 'the essence of true conversion,' says Newman, 'is a *surrender* of self, an unreserved, unconditional surrender.' Such a willingness is implied in the examples of calls in Scripture. Samuel, under Eli's instructions, promptly replied, 'Speak, Lord, for thy servant heareth,' and St Paul, when given a miraculous call, promptly replied, 'Lord, what wilt Thou have me to do?' (*PPS* V, 17, pp. 241–42; VIII, 2, pp. 17–20)

Faith and Obedience

Newman described a Christian's growth in holiness as one in faith and obedience. These words as used by Newman had a specific meaning which must be properly understood. He is not referring to acts but rather to habits. Thus, he calls faith 'a *habit,* a state of mind, lasting and consistent. To have faith in God is to surrender one's self to God, humbly to put one's interests, or to wish to be allowed to put them into His hands who is the Sovereign Giver of all good.' Elsewhere he refers to faith as an habitual living in the objects of one's faith, in the invisible world of God, Christ, the angels, and saints.

By obedience Newman means more than doing the will of God, though it includes this, but rather the earnest endeavor, knowing that one is a sinner, to please God, to approve oneself to God, by following the intimations of conscience, to do one's duty insofar as one knows it and can do it, to keep the commandments, to follow the injunctions of Scripture.

Consequently, though distinct in idea, faith and obedience represent one state of mind: 'viewed as sitting at Jesus' feet, it is called *faith;* viewed as running to do His will it is called *obedience.*' In short, this disposition 'is the *surrender* of ourselves to our Maker in all things—supreme devotion, resignation of our will, the turning with all our heart to God; and this state of mind is ascribed in Scripture sometimes to the believing, some-times the obedient, according to the particular passage,' as Newman proceeded to illustrate.

These two words therefore refer to the total surrender of one's being to the purification of the inner man, especially of his affections, separating him from an inordinate love of the world, so that one grows in a sense of one's own unworthiness before God, takes delight in prayer and in the will of God as expressed in Scripture, and recognizes the world as a veil which must be pierced so that the soul may hold concourse with the invis-ible world. Good works, on their part, obedience to the prescriptions of Scripture, form habits and attitudes of mind, which in turn sever the soul from the world of sense. (*PPS* III, sermon 6; I, 1, p. 9; *CS,* pp. 65–66)

Faith and obedience therefore are not static but dynamic, grown into, matured. It is impossible, Newman remarks, 'to endure and feed upon the gospel-doctrines all at once. . . . The most one can do is to *desire* to believe them . . . to persevere in obedience, so that little by little our souls may be changed into the abiding image of His Son.' (MS sermon no. 205)

Newman constantly emphasized the need of obedience, especially in the first volume of *Parochial and Plain Sermons,* because he thought the Evangelicals in stressing faith neglected the details of obedience. They concentrated on St Paul's declaration that man is justified by faith and not by good works, while ignoring the rest of Scripture which enjoins obe-dience, such as Our Lord's assurance, 'He will reward every man accord-ing to his works'; St Paul's, that 'we must all appear before the Judgment-seat of Christ, that every one may receive the things done in his body, according to that he hath done, whether it be good or bad'; St Peter's, that 'He is ordained of God to be the Judge of quick and dead'; St James', that 'a man is justified by works and not by faith only'; and St John's, that 'they are blessed that do His commandments, that they might have right to the tree of life, and may enter in through the gates into the city.' (*PPS* III, 6, pp. 87–88; II, pp. 153ff.)

Newman's concept of faith is also biblical in that it implies trust as well as acceptance of supernatural realities. (*PPS* I, 15, p. 191) It is therefore intimately linked with trust in God's personal providence over the individual soul.

God's Providence over the Individual

Newman had an enormous appreciation and understanding of God's providence not only over his own life but also over that of all other human beings. Having become man God in his mercy regards and consults for each individual. His mercy 'has the particular shade and mode of feeling for each, and on some men it so bestows itself, as if He depended for His own happiness on their well being.' And so Newman made a valiant attempt to bring this truth home to his hearers in a passage that has lost none of its freshness for having become classic:

> God beholds thee individually, whoever thou art. He 'calls thee by thy name.' He sees thee, and understands thee, as He made thee. He knows what is in thee, all thy own peculiar feelings and thoughts, thy dispositions and likings, thy strength and thy weakness. He views thee in thy day of rejoicing, and thy day of sorrow. He sympathizes in thy hopes and thy temptations. He interests Himself in all thy anxieties and remembrances, all the risings and failing of thy spirit. . . . Thou dost not love thyself better than He loves thee. Thou canst not shrink from pain more than He dislikes thy bearing it; and if He puts it on thee, it is as thou wilt put it on thyself, if thou art wise, for a greater good afterwards. Thou art not only His creature (though for the very sparrows He has a care, and pitied the 'much cattle' of Nineveh), thou art man redeemed and sanctified, His adopted son, favoured with a portion of that glory and blessedness which flows from Him everlastingly unto the Only-begotten. Thou was one of those for whom Christ offered up His last prayer, and sealed it with His precious blood. (*PPS* III, 9, p. 125)

It is not easy, however, to discern when God addressed us, and what He says. Even religious men who on the whole believe that His providence is guiding them and blessing them personally, 'yet when they attempt to put their finger upon the times and places, the traces of His presence disappear.' (PPS VI, 17, p. 248) Newman often emphasized that the daily providences of God are generally not recognized until later. 'Events happen to us pleasant or painful; we do not know at the time the meaning of them, we do not see God's hand in them. If indeed we have faith, we confess what we do not see, and take all that happens as His. We see nothing.' He thought this a general principle derived from Scripture, and he cited the examples of Jacob and Joseph: 'Jacob cried out on one occasion, "All these things are against me;" certainly so they seemed to be. One son made away with by the rest, another in prison in a foreign land. . . . Yet all these things were working for good.' So too with Joseph in Egypt, tempted, overcoming it, cast into prison, the iron entering into his soul, waiting there for the Lord to be gracious. Though it was constantly said, the Lord was with Joseph, apparently all things were against him. 'Yet afterwards he saw, what was so mysterious at the time;—"God did send me before you," he said to his brethren, "to preserve life. . . . It was not you that sent me hither, but God; and He hath made me a father to Pharaoh, and lord of all his house, and a ruler throughout all the land of Egypt."' (PPS IV, 17, pp. 258–59)

One must accustom oneself constantly to be looking out for evidence of God's providence in the ordinary matters of the day. 'This is what thoughtful persons come to believe, and they begin to have a sort of faith in the Divine meaning of the accidents (as they are called) of life, and a readiness to take impressions from them, which may easily become excessive, and which, whether excessive or not, is sure to be ridiculed by the world at large as superstition.' Since, however, Scripture tells us all things work together for our good, 'it does certainly encourage us in thus looking out for His presence in every thing that happens, however trivial, and in holding that to religious ears even the bad world prophesies of Him.' (PPS VI, 17, pp. 249–50) Newman was aware of the danger of faith becoming superstitious, but on the whole he believed it better to err in this direction than in the direction of rationalism or skepticism. 'Taking human nature as it is, we may surely concede a little superstition, as not the worst of evils, if it be the price of making sure of faith.'

It is difficult therefore for a Christian especially in his early years to see where divine providence is leading him. This is because God is most gracious. He leads little by little. 'He does not show you whither He is leading you; you might be frightened did you see the whole prospect at once.' Newman was keenly conscious of the hopes and desires of the young: 'I can well believe that you have hopes now, which you cannot give up, and even which support you in your present course. Be it so; whether they will be fulfilled, or not, is in His hand. He may be pleased to grant the desires of your heart; if so, thank Him for His mercy; only be sure, that all will be for your highest good.' Trust, complete and utter trust, is an essential ingredient in following the Providence of God. (*PPS* I, 26, pp. 348–49)

Motivation

To grow in holiness one must have a singleness of purpose. Few, however, do what is right 'because God tells them; they have another aim; the desire to please self or man. . . . One man loves to be at ease, another to be busy, another to enjoy domestic comfort.' Thus, instead of being primary religion is but secondary in their lives. (*PPS* I, 3, p. 39) Since men in general operate on mixed motives, one of the tasks of a Christian is to purify his motives. (*PPS* III, 15, p. 214) The love of Christ must inform all the actions of the Christian in all his acquisition of various virtues. 'If you would do works meet for penance, they must proceed from a living flame of charity. If you would secure perseverance to the end, you must gain it by continual loving prayer to the Author and Finisher of faith and obedience. If you would have a good prospect of His acceptance of you in your last moments, still it is love alone which secures His love, and blots out sin. . . . Nothing but charity can enable you to live well or to die well.' (*Mix.*, p. 80) Even self-denial and fasting require this motivation. 'If we fast, without uniting ourselves in heart to Christ . . . we fast as Jews, not as Christians.' Fasting is but one means of subduing ourselves to Christ. (*PPS* VI, 1, p. 3)

For Newman Balaam was a prime example of a high-principled, conscientious man, and yet on the side of God's enemies, because he lacked pure motives. He obeyed God from a sense of its being right to do so, 'but not from a *desire to please Him,* not from *fear and love.* . . . His endeavour was, not to please God, but to please self without displeasing

God; to pursue his own ends *as far* as was consistent with his duty.'
Newman saw this type of character on all sides of him in the society of his
day: 'moral, without being religious.' (*PPS* IV, 2, pp. 28–30) They were
obedient to conscience in its moral, not in its religious modality.

The purest motive in serving God is love of God and love of man for
His sake, but few persons—even the most religiously inclined—would
deny, if they are honest with themselves, that they in fact fall short of this
ideal. At one extreme are those for whom religion is a principle which
interferes with their enjoyments unintelligibly and irrationally. Religion,
as far as they conceive it, 'is a system destitute of the objects of love; a
system of fear. It repels and forbids, . . . and is unnatural.' Newman
admits that this sort of fear, or really dread, *is* unnatural, but true religion
'consists of love *and* fear.' They give their fear to God and their love to
mammon. At the other end are those who strive to serve God but still fall
short of love. The greatest sacrifices without love are nothing. So too
remorse, regret, and self-reproach may show a conviction of reason, but
not a conversion of heart. A lack of love is often manifested in an indis-
position toward prayer and other exercises of devotion.

The cause of this lack of love Newman attributes to the comforts of
life. 'A smooth and easy life, an uninterrupted enjoyment of the goods of
Providence, full meals, soft raiment, well-furnished homes, the pleasures
of sense, the feeling of security, the consciousness of wealth—these, and
the like, if we are not careful, choke up all the avenues of the soul,
through which the light and breath of heaven might come to us.' A hard
life, Newman cautions, does not in itself produce spiritual fruits. Nevertheless, 'we must, at least at seasons, defraud ourselves of nature, if we
would not be defrauded of grace.'

The remedy for this deficiency in love is to maintain a constant sense
of the love of Christ dying on the cross for our salvation. Moreover,
Newman advises us to dwell upon the great gifts of grace given us from
infancy, the answers to prayers, the gifts He has given to His Church, His
fidelity to the new covenant, His providence over His people, how saints
have been brought to their perfection in the darkest times. By such
thoughts our service, prayers, and intercourse with men will become
imbued with the spirit of gratitude. 'Then it is that we mix with the
world without loving it, for our affections are given to one another. . . .
We are patient in bereavement, adversity, or pain, for they are Christ's
tokens.' (*PPS* V, sermons 6 and 23)

Newman expanded and developed this theme of gratitude in another sermon, 'Remembrance of Past Mercies.' In it he declares that David, Jacob, and St Paul are presented to us in Scripture as the three great patterns of thankfulness. Just as faith was Abraham's distinguishing grace, so Jacob's special characteristic 'was a habit of affectionate musing upon God's providences towards him in times past, and of overflowing thankfulness for them.' As St Paul urged his fellow Christians to give thanks always to God with great joy, so Newman exhorted his hearers,

> Let us humbly and reverently attempt to trace His guiding hand in the years which we have hitherto lived. Let us thankfully commemorate the many mercies He has vouchsafed to us in time past, the many sins He has not remembered, the many dangers He has averted, the many prayers He has answered, the many mistakes He has corrected, the many warnings, the many lessons, the much light, the abounding comfort which He has from time to time given. (*PPS* V, sermon 6)

Another most important motive is to maintain a constant love of holiness, a motive Newman insists upon again and again. It is the only way to prepare for eternal life, to overcome the attractions of the world, to progress toward achieving the aim to which we are called and for which we have been created. (*PPS* I, sermon 1) Anyone who wishes to serve God and to grow in holiness has to face two formidable enemies: sin and the world. Why this is so will be explored in the following three chapters.

Notes

1. See above, pp. 12ff.
2. 'Remarks on the Covenant of Grace, in connection with the Doctrine of Election, Baptism, and the Church, 1828?' BOA.
3. Newman came to realize that his own 'first' conversion was in fact 'a returning to, a renewing of, principles, under the power of the Holy Spirit, which I had already felt, and in a measure acted on, when young.' (*AW*, p. 172)
4. Conscience is frequently mentioned in Newman's writings: *PPS* I, 15, pp. 201–2; I, 17, pp. 216–17; *OS*, sermon 5; *US*, 2, pp. 18–19; but the fullest treatment is in *GA*, pp. 105ff. and *Diff.* II, pp. 248ff.

Chapter Two

Sin and Its Aftermath

MAN HAS become alienated from God by reason of sin. What is sin and what is its malice and effects upon the character? Newman's understanding of sin seems to have been determined by his own personal experience, by the Calvinism of the authors he read but whose doctrine he modified, and finally by the accounts of sin in the Old Testament. It was especially from the latter that he recognized sin as rebellion against God, and from the Calvinists that it flowed from man's fallen human nature as they understood it.

In referring to his youthful experience of sin, he said, 'I was terrified at the heavy hand of God which came down upon me.' A subsequent description of the feelings that accompany acts against conscience gives a partial insight into this experience, namely, 'feelings of guilt, remorse, fear of future punishment and of evils that may beset one in consequence of one's acts.' But there was much more. There was a recognition that these acts were not simply immoral but against a supreme Being, and therefore irreligious. They were 'sins.' (*GA*, pp. 105ff.; *US*, 6, pp. 105–7; *PPS* II, 2, p. 18)

Analyzing sin in various sermons, Newman affirmed that in essence sin 'is rebellion against God. . . . Sin is the mortal enemy of the All-holy, so that He and it cannot be together, and as the All-holy drives it from His presence into the outer darkness, so, if God could be less than God, it is sin that would have the power to make Him less.' (*Mix.*, 16, p. 335) Sin is disobedience, insubordination, the refusal to submit to the will of God, when one comes to know it in conscience. It is the rejection of God's dominion. Newman sometimes referred to this as 'wilfulness.' It was the sin of Saul. He preferred to do his own will rather than God's, in his way rather than in God's way. (*PPS* III, sermon 3; *US,* sermon 9)

Sin is not merely immorality, the acting against a system of laws or a code of moral principles. Balaam tried to act from a sense of right, rather than from love and fear, but he is not alone in this respect. All men are inclined to do the same. 'We are apt to act towards God and the things of God as towards a mere system, a law, a name, a religion, a principle, not as against a Person, a living, watchful, present, prompt and powerful Eye and Arm.' (*PPS* IV, 2, p. 31) That is to say, one is likely to recognize conscience as a moral sense but not in its religious modality. This was the weakness of what Newman called in the *Idea of a University,* 'the religion of civilization,' and in a sermon, 'the Religion of the Day.' (*Idea,* pp. 182ff.; *PPS* I, sermon 14)

Knowledge and realization of the intrinsic evil of sin are not easy to acquire, for they depend upon a knowledge of the majesty and infinite dignity and holiness of God. 'We do not know what sin is, because we do not know what God is. . . . Only God's glories, His perfections, His holiness, His Majesty, His beauty, can teach us by the contrast how to think of sin.' (*Mix.,* 2, p. 33) Nor do we fully recognize ourselves objectively as we stand in God's sight as sinners until we appreciate His infinite Holiness. 'It is the sight of God, revealed to the eye of faith, that makes us hideous to ourselves, from the contrast which we find ourselves to present to that great God. . . . It is the vision of Him in His infinite gloriousness, the All-holy, the All-beautiful, the All-perfect, which makes us sink into the earth with self-contempt and self-abhorrence.' (*OS,* 2, p. 27) Such was the feeling of St Peter when he fell on his knees and cried out, 'Depart from me, for I am a sinful man.' This too was the feeling of holy Job, when he heard God speak. Even though he had served God for many years, he said, 'But now my eye seeth Thee; therefore I reprove myself, and do penance in dust and ashes.' So it was with Daniel, Isaias, St Paul, and Mary Magdalen. It is the recognition of what God is and what one's self is by contrast that issues in humility.

Only at the judgment will man come to a full realization of the horror of sin because God is more clearly known. 'Then will the good man undergo the full sight of his sins, which on earth he was labouring to obtain, and partly succeeded in obtaining, though life was not long enough to learn and subdue them all.' (*PPS* I, 4, p. 48) As he wrote in the

Dream of Gerontius through the mouth of the guardian angel speaking to
Gerontius,

> There is a pleading in His pensive eyes
> Will pierce thee to the quick, and trouble thee.
> And thou will hate and loathe thyself; for, though
> Now sinless, thou wilt feel that thou has sinn'd
> As never thou didst feel; and wilt desire
> To slink away and hide thee from His sight.   (*VV*, p. 359)

Since sin in itself is irrational, it is sometimes called in Scripture
'madness.' 'As literal madness is derangement of the reason, so sin is
derangement of the heart, of the Spirit, of the affections.' (*CS*, pp. 83–84)
Why then does man sin? First, sin though forbidden is often attractive
and pleasurable. (*PPS* VII, 13, p. 181) Second, curiosity to experience the
pleasures of sin prompt to disobedience. 'Not to know sin by experience
brings upon a man the laughter and jests of his companions.' It is a snare
Satan uses to entrap so as eventually to enslave men. (*PPS* VIII, 5, pp.
63–65; *CS*, p. 76) Third, not the least attraction is the feeling that it
brings about 'an enlargement of mind' and a development of the person.
Referring no doubt to his own early experiences, Newman remarks that
when someone first listens to the arguments and speculations of unbe-
lievers, he feels 'what is a very novel light they cast upon what he has
hitherto accounted most sacred.' Sins to which the young are tempted
'excite the curiosity of the innocent, and they intoxicate the imagination,'
so that their 'eyes seem opened upon a new world, from which they look
back upon their state of innocence with a sort of pity and contempt, as if
it were below the dignity of men.' (*US*, 14, p. 284)

Once sin has been experienced, the sinner is led by an inner dyna-
mism, unless checked by the power of grace, to further sins, as Newman
illustrated in a sermon on Jeroboam. His first sin was to rise up against
Solomon, then against Solomon's son, and then he became idolatrous in
order to maintain his kingdom. 'When a man begins to do wrong, he
cannot answer for himself how far he may be carried on. He does not see
beforehand, he cannot know where he shall find himself after the sin is
committed. One false step forces him to another, for retreat is impossible.' (*PPS* III, 5, p. 67; *CS*, pp. 110–11)

Original Sin

Newman's interest in the phenomenology of sin led him to explore the source of sin in the interior depths of a man's soul. Personal knowledge of oneself provides evidence which makes the doctrine of original sin and redemption commend itself to reason. How does man come to this evidence? It is through trying to follow his conscience. 'Wishing then and striving to act up to the law of conscience, he will yet find that, with his utmost efforts, and after his most earnest prayers, he still falls short of what he knows to be right, and what he aims at. . . . Thus he will learn from experience the doctrine of original sin, before he knows the actual name of it.' (*PPS* VIII, 8, pp. 116–17) To be sure, without revelation one cannot know the doctrine of Adam's fall and the loss of supernatural grace, but a man in striving to follow conscience will experience within himself a principle which is at odds with what God wills.

In his sermons Newman did not explore the nature of original sin, about which he is at times vague; rather he was concerned about its effects. He makes no distinction between the tendency to sin as an effect of original sin and original sin itself. He rather concentrated on impressing on his hearers that sin arises from what he called an evil principle within us. In an early sermon 'On the Corruption of Human Nature,' he declines to discuss the extent of man's corruption, whether total or partial, but concentrates on showing how men in the concrete despite their best efforts actually sin and how great sins man is prone to and will commit unless prevented by the grace of God. This argues to the truth that our very nature is at fault.[1]

In a subsequent sermon preached in 1832 he remarks on the importance of the doctrine of original sin: 'It is very humbling. . . . Men can without trouble be brought to confess that they sin, i.e. that they commit sins. . . . But they do not like to be told that the race from which they proceed is degenerate. . . . They think they *can* do their duty, *only do not choose to do it*; they like to believe . . . that they do not want assistance.' (*PPS* I, 7, p. 87)

As a result of the fall, man experiences an internal disharmony which did not exist before Adam's fall. He does not have the control over his feelings which Adam had at first. 'Adam, before his fall, felt, we may suppose, love, fear, hope, joy, dislike, as we do now; but he felt them only when he ought, and as he ought; all was harmoniously attempered and rightly adjusted in his soul, which was at unity with itself. But, at the fall, this beautiful order and peace was broken up; the same passions remained, but their use and action were changed; they rushed into extremes, sometimes excessive, sometimes the reverse. Indignation was corrupted into wrath; self-love became selfishness, self-respect became pride and emulation envy and jealousy. They were at variance with each other; pride struggled with self-interest, fear with desire. Thus his soul became a chaos.' (*PPS* VII, 4, p. 43; V, 8, p. 114)

Man's inner unity has been destroyed, so that not only does he not have complete control over his feelings as Adam once had, but his faculties are at variance with each other. As a result, when he comes to the age of reason he becomes conscious of these divisions within: 'appetite, passion, secular ambition, intellect, and conscience, all trying severally to get possession of him. . . . And thus, at least for a time, he is in a state of internal strife, confusion, and uncertainty, first attracted this way, then that, not knowing how to choose, though sooner or later choose he must; or rather, he must choose soon, and cannot choose late, for he cannot help thinking, speaking, and acting; and to think, speak and act is to choose.' (*OS* I, pp. 6–7)

At times man's intellect is at war with his conscience. Imagination too can lead astray. What his intellect tells him may not necessarily be accepted by the imagination. In the *Apologia* Newman mentions that in consequence of his reading Newton on the Prophecies, he became convinced that the Pope was Antichrist. 'My imagination was stained by the effects of this doctrine up to the year 1843; it had been obliterated from my reason and judgment at an earlier date; but the thought remained upon me as a sort of false conscience.' (*Apo.*, p. 7) So in the depths of his being man experiences opposition at times between some of his faculties, no matter how he chooses. He is like 'some musical instrument of great power and compass, but imperfect; from its very structure some keys must ever be out of tune.' (*DA*, p. 272)

Given these tendencies in man, 'the power of temptation, the force of the passions, the strength of self-love and self-will, the sovereignty of pride and sloth,' it is inevitable that he will sin and seriously unless he has an abundance of grace to prevent it. (*Mix.*, p. 8)

Such a recognition of sin and its inevitability can and should lead a person to look out for a Redeemer, if he is not a believer. If he is, he must recognize that without the continuing grace of Christ, he cannot please God, attain his eternal salvation, or integrate his faculties during his lifetime. 'Any standard of duty, which does not convict him of real and multiplied sins, and of incapacity to please God of his own strength, is untrue; and any rule of life, which leaves him contented with himself, without fear, without anxiety, without humiliation, is deceptive; it is the blind leading the blind: yet such, in one shape or other, is the religion of the whole earth, beyond the pale of the Church.' (*OS*, 5, p. 67; 2, p. 20)

The action of the Holy Spirit on the soul in baptism eliminates the curse of Adam and restores it to supernatural life, but it does not eliminate either the tendency to sin or its attraction. Man is not in a state of perfection. He is called to one, but he will not realize it without an interior struggle and conflict over a period of years. Only gradually will he be able to master his passions, to control them, and progressively to integrate his interior being and faculties. A perfect integration, however, cannot be achieved in this life. (*PPS* IV, 1, pp. 4ff.; VII, 13, p. 186)

Nevertheless, man can make progress in this life. Gradually one's tastes, judgments, and views are changed. Christian attitudes are acquired. In this way grace can achieve the destruction of the curse of sin, but it does not entirely eliminate the root of sin: the attraction of serious sin and the inevitability of minor offenses. Thus, one must undergo that continual conversion already spoken of. A religious person 'is ever taking advantage of holy seasons and new providences, and beginning again. The elements of sin are still alive within him; they still tempt and influence him, and threaten when they do no more; and it is only by a continual fight against them that he prevails; and what shall persuade him that his power to fight is his own, and not from above? And this conviction of a Divine Presence with him is stronger according to the length of time during which he has served God, and to his advance in holiness. . . . Religious men, really such, cannot but recollect in the course of years, that they have become very different from what they were.' (*SD*, 23, pp. 349–50)

Such progress in holiness and good works does not merit for the Christian the grace of perseverance which is an additional gift, for which he must pray. God grants it to us because it is necessary for our salvation, 'though He does not grant even to Saints the prerogative of avoiding every venial sin.' Again Newman emphasizes the lesson of humility and watchfulness that should be drawn from this doctrine, a doctrine that should not depress. He urges his hearers to have recourse to the various channels of grace and to pray to Mary the Mother of God. (*Mix.*, pp. 127–29, 143–44; *PPS* I, 24, pp. 323–24)

Consequences of Sin

Man inevitably sins and the first consequence of sin is the punishment that follows either in this life or in the next. To deny that sin is punished seemed to Newman a form of self-deception. (*US*, 6, pp. 111–14; *PPS* VI, 2, pp. 22–23) As far as the future life is concerned Newman did not preach purgatory in his Anglican sermons because he did not think it a revealed doctrine. He preached an intermediate state between death and the final resurrection, in which souls would not suffer but would rest in peace, though not yet admitted to heaven. This caused a problem as to how satisfaction could be made for sin. (Tract 79, *VM* II, p. 288; *PPS* III, sermon 25)

The existence of hell, that is, *eternal* punishment for sin, Newman accepted from the time of his first conversion, but, as he said in the *Apologia,* he 'tried in various ways to make that truth less terrible to reason.' (*Apo.*, p. 6) That sin involved punishment he thought man could conclude without the aid of revelation, but that the punishment was eternal was a trial of faith. It seemed to go contrary to the attribute of God's goodness, and it was difficult to imagine any man, no matter how evil, entirely devoid of any good qualities. This would seem to argue the injustice of eternal punishment for sin. (*SD*, 6, pp. 74–77)

Of the means he took to make the doctrine 'less terrible' was his conjecture that the soul in hell is not necessarily conscious of the passage of time, hence there is no increase of suffering because of duration. Second, he appealed to our ignorance of what eternity means. He pursued another approach to the truth of eternal punishment in the consideration of the relationship of the soul to God after death. A condemned soul is one who is frozen in an attitude of deliberate rejection of God. Such a person would be unhappy in heaven; he would necessarily flee from the Almighty repelled by the vision of God.[2]

Newman was also convinced that punishment for sin takes place in this life. Even if one cannot associate a definite punishment with a definite sin, still a Christian should be able to accept all suffering in his life as a punishment inflicted by the hand of God Himself. In his own life Newman applied this view not only with regard to physical pain but more especially to mental anguish and trials of the intellect. Whatever other meanings such trials may have, they are the price that is paid for disobedience to God and the rejection of His sovereign will. (*AW,* p. 121; *Moz.* II, p. 334, *KC,* p. 279; *PPS* III, 11, p. 155; VI, 2, p. 25)

To Newman as a Catholic the doctrine of purgatory opened up a vision of punishment for sin after death that was not eternal. In his analysis, the suffering of purgatory consists in the simultaneous attraction toward God and the repulsion from the sight of God and His infinite majesty. As he expressed it in the *Dream of Gerontius:*

And these two pains, so counter and so keen,—
The longing for Him, when thou seest Him not;
The shame of self at thought of seeing Him,—
Will be thy veriest, sharpest purgatory.—(*VV,* p. 360)

By this inner tension between simultaneously longing for God and recognizing its own unworthiness the soul is purified.

Sin not only brings punishment but also other consequences. The sinner, even a repentant one, is never the same as if he had never sinned. 'God may forgive, but the sin had done its work, and its memento is set up in the soul.' We never attain the perfection we should have attained had we not sinned. Newman makes this assertion; he does not seem to give reasons for it. How can one know what perfection one would have achieved? It seems to go counter to Paul's assertion, where sin abounded, grace abounded more. Did not St Paul himself and Mary Magdalen reach heights of perfection precisely through their repentance and outstanding love fed by the recollection of the mercy of Christ? The difficulty with this objection is that Newman himself recognized the cases of St Paul and St Mary Magdalen, but he does not seem to have perceived any contradiction between these two positions which he does not attempt to reconcile. (*PPS* I, 8, pp. 110–11; II, 8, pp. 99–102)

A further effect of sin is the damage it does to conscience. The innocent 'are able to discern at once the right and wrong in conduct, as by some delicate instrument which tells truly because it has never been ill-treated.' (*PPS* II, 27, p. 341) A sinful man finds it difficult to discern what is right and wrong. If conscience is disregarded, it ceases to upbraid; and thus sins, once known, become in time secret sins. Sins which once shocked are gradually forgotten. Such is the effect of habit upon the workings of conscience. Dishonesty, self-indulgence begin in acts, and terminate in a life-style which is contrary to the Gospels, while the original acts go unremembered, unrecognized, and unrepented. (*PPS* I, 4, pp. 51–53)

Most men are unaware of their secret faults. That we have faults unknown to ourselves is a fair presumption from the fact that we can see the faults of others, of which they are totally unaware. It is often only under trial or actual falling that such a fault is revealed to ourselves, as it was to St Peter, who followed Christ boldly, but did not suspect his own weakness until he had betrayed and denied Christ in the time of temptation. So in the case of men who seem to live good lives, the presumption is still valid. Only God sees these faults. 'Not *acts* alone of sin does He set down against us daily, of which we know nothing, but the thoughts of the heart too. The stirrings of pride, vanity, covetousness, impurity, discontent, resentment, these succeed each other through the day in momentary emotions, and are known to Him. We know them not; but how much it concerns us to know them.' (*PPS* I, sermon 4)

One of the most startling of Newman's assertions as to the effects of sin is that of 'judicial blindness.' As a result of youthful sins comes the temptation to rebelliousness against the authority of conscience itself and against faith. Reason led on by passion wars against one's better knowledge. As the progress in sin continues, the light of conscience is gradually withdrawn and the soul 'is left to "grope and stumble in the desolate places," by the dim, uncertain light of reason.' How far any individual proceeds in this course depends upon a variety of causes, but the most common case, says Newman, is for one to become involved in the business of life, and 'professed faith becomes a mere matter of *words*, not *ideas and principles*,' and one's opinions result from 'random and accidental use of the reasoning powers, . . . not the result of habitual, firm, and progressive obedience to God.' (*PPS* I, sermon 17)

In the case of clear and brilliant intellects their first sin is to value themselves upon their superiority of intellect, and to look down on others. They substitute reason (i.e., their reasoning powers) for conscience, valuing truths 'exactly in proportion to the possibility of proving them by means of that mere reason. Hence, moral and religious truths are thought little of by them, because they fall under the province of *Conscience* far more than of intellect. Religion sinks in their estimation. . . . As to the code of morals, they acknowledge it . . . so far as its dicta can be *proved* by reasoning, by an appeal to sight, and to expedience and without reference to a natural sense of right and wrong as the sanction of these informants. Thinking much of intellectual advancement, they are much bent on improving the world by making *all men* intellectual; and they labour to convince themselves, that as men grow in knowledge they will grow in virtue.' This was the fundamental fallacy of what Newman called 'the liberalism' of the day and of the utilitarian philosophy of education in particular, which he mercilessly exposed with irony and satire in his Letters to the *Times* on the opening of the Tamworth Reading Room. (*PPS* I, sermon 17; *DA* IV)

Character Defects as a Result of Sin

Sins affect not only the working of conscience and one's principles; they affect a person's character as well. Newman concluded that long-forgotten sins of childhood and of youth produce inconsistencies in the character of otherwise good men. This is the reason why there are so few saints. Defects of character are often buried in people and account for why they turn out differently than expected, for example, when a person attains to a position of power. Moreover, single sins indulged in or neglected are often the cause of other defects of character, which seem to have no connection with them. This is commonly acknowledged with regard to a skeptical cast of mind. Questioning one's faith has often its root, not in reasoning or intellectual difficulties, but in moral faults, however much the person tries to disassociate the two. This holds true, says Newman, in other cases. 'Softness of mind and manner and false refinement may sometimes be the result of allowing ourselves impure thoughts; or wanderings in prayer may have some subtle connexion with self-conceit; or passionateness may owe its power over us to indulgence, though without excess, in eating and drinking.' Newman is not asserting that these sins are related by means of cause and effect, but stating a connection which holds at times in matter of fact, however it is accounted for.

Looking at the same phenomenon from another point of view, Newman affirms that there are few persons but have some 'besetting sin or other, some infirmity, temptation, and in resisting these lies their trial.' Newman himself, it will be recalled from the entries in his diary, struggled hard against his unspecified besetting sin. Consequently, a man may be religious except for this one infirmity, which he may be unaware of, but which nevertheless is affecting his character. Some youthful sins bring great remorse and guilt feelings so that one cannot but help being aware of them; 'they strike no secret blow.' Far different is it with covetousness, conceit, ambition, or resentment. These are easily disguised and though they affect the conscience momentarily, the pang is soon over. Newman takes the example of a person who otherwise experiences an inner harmony, but is given to resentful thoughts which jar the mind like one string out of tune. 'Some particular person has injured him or dishonoured him, and a few minutes of each day or of each week are given to indulging harsh, unforgiving thoughts which at first he suspected were what they really are, sinful, but which he gradually learned to palliate, or no longer recognizes as sinful, yet they are having an effect upon him.' (PPS IV, sermon 3)

Self-Knowledge

The remedy to cure these faults begins with self-knowledge of both the conscious and subconscious life. But perhaps what is more important is that unless one has such a knowledge, one's understanding of the doctrine of *forgiveness* of sins, of a *new birth* from sin, is *unreal*. 'We shall be using words without attaching [a] distinct meaning to them. Thus self-knowledge is at the root of *real* religious knowledge. . . . For it is in proportion as we search our hearts and understand our own nature, that we understand what is meant by an Infinite Governor and Judge; in proportion as we comprehend the nature of disobedience and our actual sinfulness, that we feel what is the blessing of the removal of sin, redemption, pardon, sanctification, which otherwise are mere words. God speaks primarily in our hearts.'

Self-knowledge, however, is not easily gained because self-examination of one's principles and motives is difficult, painful, and takes times. Self-love makes us satisfied with a general acknowledgment of our faults and sins and a contentment with self, especially if one enjoys good health, is cheerful, and is happy in one's family life. Perhaps the most frequent obstacle, as has been said, is the force of habit. We gradually forget wrongs which once shocked us, because we have gotten used to them. For example, the duty of stated prayer is omitted with compunction, but soon with indifference. Then too the force of contemporary opinion and fashion influences us unconsciously.

Our *first* principles are especially difficult to uncover, because they are ordinarily not known and recognized as such. Newman explained why: 'They are hidden for the very reason they are so sovereign and so engrossing. They have sunk into you; they spread through you; you do not so much appeal to them as act from them. And this in great measure is meant by saying that self-knowledge is so difficult; that is, in other words, men commonly do not know their First Principles.' When these first principles are taken together, they form the personality and character of the individual. They rule him and are not ruled in turn. They are the guides in speculation, deliberation, decision-making, and action. They may be true or false, but either way, 'they are the condition of our mental life; by them we form our view of events, or deeds, or persons, of lines of conduct, of aims, of moral qualities, of religions. They constitute the difference between man and man; they characterize him . . . they are, in short, the man.' (*Prepos.*, pp. 283–84)

A man is responsible for his religious and moral first principles. Consequently, by disregarding the dictates of conscience, a man's character is formed without his ever realizing this is taking place. 'But there are *ways* of unlearning them when they are false.' (*Prepos.*, p. 279) Self-examination is one of the ways, but even if one perseveres in prayer and self-examination, one will never get to the bottom of the heart. Only at the final judgment will the depths of the heart be fully revealed. (*CS*, p. 36) 'To think of these things, and to be alarmed, is the first step towards acceptable obedience; to be at ease, is to be unsafe. We must know what the evil of sin is hereafter, if we do not learn it here.' (*PPS* I, sermon 4; I, 24, p. 323)

Notes

1. As a Catholic Newman contrasted the Protestant and Catholic views of original sin: the former placed original sin in a corruption of nature, the latter in the privation of supernatural grace. (*LD* XIX, pp. 361–70; *Diff*. II, pp. 44–50) Nevertheless it is difficult simply to affirm that as an Anglican he held the Protestant view especially in his later years. In his lectures on justification and notes on St Athanasius he proposed the Catholic view, but in the *PPS* there is no clear assertion. Though he apparently discarded the total corruption of nature, his statements seem to consider original sin as some form of corruption of nature which remains. As late as December 1841 he still preached an early sermon, no. 19, 'On the Corruption of Human Nature,' though he omitted and modified some statements.

In this sermon Newman affirms that there is a principle of disobedience which is not an accident of our nature, but rooted in it, and he asserts that the holiest of men were witnesses to their own 'innate corruption.' He then quotes Bishop Beveridge: 'I do not only betray the inbred venom of my heart by poisoning my common actions but even my most religious performances also, with sin. I cannot pray, but I sin—nay I cannot hear or preach a sermon, but I sin—I cannot give an alms or receive the sacrament but I sin—nay, I cannot so much as confess my sins, but my very confessions are still aggravations of them. My repentance needs to be repented of.'

The statements on original sin in his published sermons are not always clear and consistent. In one sermon, he quoted the ninth of the Thirty-Nine Articles about the corruption of human nature and from the same article the statement, 'the Apostle doth confess that concupiscence and lust hath of itself the nature of sin.' (*PPS* V, p. 90) Because of this Newman as a Catholic would not allow this sermon in Copeland's selection, and admitted its harshness, nor would he allow no. 9 in Volume 5, because of the assertions on p. 120, 'the body of death which infects us, . . . sins because it *is* sin.' (*LD* XXVIII, p. 250)

Certainly the impression created by some of the sermons on sin is pretty grim, owing, it seems, to the Calvinistic tradition. On the other hand, it has likewise to be acknowledged that Newman approaches St Augustine in his recognition of the subtle self-deceptions and treacheries of the human heart, as well as of the opposition human nature instinctively puts up to the requirements of humility, self-sacrifice, and all 'the hard things' that Christian perfection demands. Like Augustine he too saw that true perfection reaches into the sub-conscious and requires not only grace but a lifetime vigilance, control of one's emotions, appetites and instincts, as well as a continual self-examination of one's actions and motives.

2. N to J. M. Capes, 2 December 1849, *LD* XIII, pp. 318–19; *GA*, p. 502; *SE*, p. 86; *PPS* I, 1, pp. 1–8; *Call.*, pp. 219ff.

Chapter Three

The Christian Response to Sin

INSOFAR AS sin is a reality in the life of a Christian, he can never eliminate entirely from his spiritual life fear of God and of offending Him. To the knowledge of sin rendered by his conscience the Christian adds from the Old and New Testaments a knowledge of the condemnation, the warnings against sin and its consequences. For Newman this remained a lifetime conviction. [1] This fear is not only a fear of punishment but a reverential fear of offending the Infinite Almighty God and Moral Governor. Hence, during his lifetime the Christian cannot serve God without fear, if he has any real apprehension of God as He is and of himself as he really is. Indeed, it is the Creator Spirit 'who brings into religion the true devotion, the true worship, and changes the self-satisfied Pharisee into the broken-hearted, self-abased Publican.' (*OS,* 2, pp. 26–27). Only after death will fear be eliminated, and this because the Christian feared in this life. As Newman expressed it so clearly in the *Dream of Gerontius:*

> SOUL
>   Dear Angel, say,
> Why have I now no fear at meeting Him?
> Along my earthly life, the thought of death
> And judgment was to me most terrible.
> I had it aye before me, and I saw
> The Judge severe e'en in the Crucifix.
> Now that the hour is come, my fear is fled;
> And at this balance of my destiny,
> Now close upon me, I can forward look
> With a serenest joy.

ANGEL
      It is because
Then thou didst fear, that now thou dost not fear,
Thou hast forestall'd the agony, and so
For thee the bitterness of death is past.   (*VV*, pp. 341–42)

Nor is fear incompatible with the command of love as the essential note of our relationship with God and Christ. 'In heaven, love will absorb fear; but in this world *fear and love must go together.* No one can love God aright without fearing Him; though many fear Him, and yet do not love Him. . . . Deliberate sinners fear but cannot love Him.' Even in human relationships reverence and respect for the other play an essential role: 'No one really loves another, who does not feel a certain reverence toward him. . . . It is mutual respect which makes friendship lasting. . . . We cannot understand Christ's mercies till we understand His power, His glory, His unspeakable holiness, and our demerits; that is, until we first fear Him. Not that fear comes first, and then love; for the most part they proceed together. Fear is allayed by the love of Him, and our love sobered by the fear of Him. Thus He draws us on with encouraging voice amid the terrors of His threatenings.' (*PPS* I, 23, pp. 303–4; see also *PPS* I, 24, p. 322)

As an Anglican Newman felt it was necessary to stress this aspect of Christianity because it was neglected in what he called 'The Religion of the Day,' though he also thought the lack of fear more universal than a mere contemporary phenomenon. He recognized a type of religion which the refined intellect of man in any age would be tempted to create in place of authentic Christianity. Instead of the full harmony of the Christian religion, with its delicate balance of opposites, it seizes upon the brighter aspects of religion and substitutes an outward show of respectability for the inward monitor of conscience. We are told that 'strait is the gate and narrow the way that leads to life, and few there be that find it,' and that those who do not obtain eternal life 'shall go into everlasting punishment.' 'This is the dark side of religion; and the men I have been describing cannot bear to think of it. They shrink from it as too terrible. . . . Conscience has been silenced. The only information they have received concerning God has been from Natural Theology, and that speaks only of benevolence and harmony; so they will not credit the plain words of

Scripture.' (*PPS* I, 23, pp. 318–19) When Samuel Wilberforce criticized Newman's first volume of *Parochial Sermons* because it was 'not quickening and encouraging—that it on the whole induces fear, and depression,' Newman replied, '*I grant it.* It was meant to do so. *We require the "Law's stern fires."*'[2]

Nor does fear eliminate joy in the life of the Christian. 'Joy and gladness are also characteristics of him, according to the exhortation in the text, "Rejoice in the Lord always," and this in spite of the fear and awe which the thought of the Last Day ought to produce in him. It is by means of these strong contrasts that Scripture brings out to us what is the real meaning of its separate portions. If we had been told merely to fear, we should have mistaken a slavish dread, or the gloom of despair, for godly fear; and if we had been told merely to rejoice, we should perhaps have mistaken a rude freedom and familiarity for joy; but when we are told both to fear and to rejoice, we gain thus much at first sight, that our joy is not to be irreverent, nor our fear to be desponding; that though both feelings are to remain, neither is to be what it would be by itself.' Nevertheless only experience can teach the Christian how concretely to combine these seemingly opposite traits: 'how joy and fear can be reconciled, words cannot show. . . . Let a man try both to fear and to rejoice, as Christ and His Apostles tell him, and in time he will learn how; but when he has learned, he will be as little able to explain how it is he does both, as he was before.' (*PPS* V, 5, pp. 65–66)

Repentance

Man by reason of sin is alienated from God. How is he to become reconciled to Him? In relinquishing Evangelicalism Newman repudiated the notion of a one-time conversion from which time he seeks God and serves Him faithfully. He came to accept rebirth in baptism and the forgiveness of sin both original and actual, if the latter exist. But post-baptismal sins must also be repented of. They cannot be forgiven without sorrow, regret, and the purpose of amendment. Consequently, persons living in sin should never postpone repentance. (*PPS* VI, 2)

What is the nature of repentance? Newman took the prodigal son as *the* type of repentance. (*PPS* III, sermon 7) First, the prodigal son says, 'I am no more worthy to be called Thy son, make me as one of Thy hired servants.' Though God's service is perfect freedom, this is so only in the case of those who have served Him for a long time. It is the happiness of the saints in heaven to take pleasure in their duty, and this is the state to which we are tending; but in the beginning religion is necessarily almost a task and a formal service. Going to church, praying in private, reading the Scriptures are in great measure a form and a task. They are wearisome. Consequently, one's initial obedience is that of a servant.

The neophyte must continually strive and pray that he may enter into the real *spirit* of these services, so that gradually he turns from a servant into a son. Though from the beginning he must turn to Christ in love, still his love may frighten 'while it encourages us, from the thought of our ingratitude. It will fill us with remorse and dread of judgment, for we have received privileges, and have abused them.'

With what motives should the penitent endeavor now to serve and please God? One of the most natural and spontaneous thoughts will be to propitiate Him. In a serious breach between friends, we sometimes try to get someone to mediate, but we also try either humble confession of being at fault or offer some acceptable service. So in various religions repentant sinners have attempted to win God's attention and engage His favor by some sort of sacrifice. In the Old Testament 'Jacob was instructed to sacrifice on the altar of Bethel, after his return from Padan-aram. David, on the other hand, speaks of the more spiritual sacrifice in the fifty-first Psalm: "The sacrifices of God are a broken spirit; a broken and a contrite heart, O God, Thou wilt not despise."'[3]

In the parable of the prodigal son we find no mention of any propitiatory work, but one of total and *unconditional surrender*. This, Newman affirms, is the noblest type of repentance and is acquired only in time. When a person first turns to God, though there is something of simple surrender, still 'the wish of appeasing God on the one hand, or a hard-hearted insensibility about our sins on the other, mere selfish dread of punishment, or the expectation of a sudden easy pardon, these, and such-like principles, influence us, whatever we may say or may think we feel.' Only after the experience of the imperfection of all out attempts to serve God will we acquiesce in a complete surrender to God, with 'more or less hope of pardon, as the case may be.' No one can be certain that he is in the state of grace, and when he looks back on the numberless omissions of duty, he can only cast himself completely on God and on the mercy of Christ. Especially 'he acknowledges and adopts, as far as he can, St. Paul's words, and nothing beyond them, "This is a faithful saying, and worthy of all acceptation, that Christ Jesus came into the world to save *sinners*, of whom I am chief."'

Since man continues to sin one way or another he must continuously practice repentance, and with time his repentance grows stronger and stronger. It becomes habitual. This is what traditional spiritual writers referred to as compunction. It is an essential element in the progress of the Christian toward holiness and perfection. No matter how holy he becomes, he can never forget that he is in *deed* a sinner and also carries within him the *tendency* to sin. The lives of the saints give plentiful witness to this truth. St Philip, for example, when going to communion would protest that he was good for nothing, but to do evil. St Rose, even when very young, subjected herself to extreme penances. 'Others may look up to them, but they ever look up to God; others may speak of their merits, but they only speak of their defects.' (*OS,* 2, pp. 16–17)

To those who have sinned grievously Newman recommended that they never 'forget they *have* sinned; if they forget it not, God in mercy *will* forget it.' They should practice daily recollection of their sins, unless it makes them sin afresh to do so, 'to confess them again and again with great shame, and entreat His pardon.' Moroever, they should look upon all pain and sorrow that comes their way as a punishment for what they once were, and 'to take it patiently on that account, nay, joyfully, as giving them a hope that God *is* punishing them here instead of hereafter.' It is better to do penance in this life than to postpone it to the next. In an age which was trying to multiply comforts and to rid life of daily inconveniences and discomforts, Newman urged penance especially during the season of Lent. 'Give back some of God's gifts to God, that you may safely enjoy the rest. Fast, or watch, or abound in alms, or be instant in prayer, or deny yourselves society, or pleasant books, or easy clothing, or take on you some irksome task or employment.' (*PPS* VI, sermon 2)

Forgiveness of Sin

The remission of postbaptismal sins remained a problem to Newman as long as he was an Anglican. He recognized the conflicting doctrines of the

Thirty-Nine Articles and the Book of Common Prayer. Though he heard confessions upon request, he did so with great reluctance, as he was not sure of the nature of absolution.[4] Consequently, he rarely speaks of confession in his sermons and when he does so, it seems in a vague way. A statement in the *Via Media* sums up his uncertainty: 'We do not know when it is that forgiveness is formally conveyed to individual Christians who have lapsed into sin, whether it is in this life, or upon death, or during the intermediate state, or at the day of judgment.' (*VM* I, p. 94; *PPS* IV, p. 114; V, 13, p. 186. See also *PPS* IV, 3, p. 38 for an example of vagueness.)

Moreover, in speaking of sin Newman does not make the distinction between mortal and venial sin. He did, however, make a distinction between serious sins and less grievous sins, the former called 'transgressions,' the latter, 'infirmities.' In the examples he gives it is clear that infirmities are owing to a lack of full consent on the part of the sinner. There is no acknowledgment of the possibility of a sin that would be venial, that is, not serious, to which full consent would be given. As examples of transgressions he cites habits of vices, quoting St Paul: 'Neither fornicators, nor idolators, nor adulterers nor effeminate nor drunkards, shall inherit the kingdom of God.' He also mentions profaneness, heresy, serious breaches of the law of charity, and hardness of heart. All these destroy the presence of grace in the soul. (*PPS* V, sermon 14)

Newman gives examples of infirmities, which do not destroy grace but lead to transgressions if not checked: (1) the remains of original sin, involuntary movements of pride, profaneness, deceit, unbelief, selfishness, greediness, etc.; (2) those which arise from our former habits of sin, though now long abandoned; sins arising from want of self-command, for example, anger, sloth, cowardice; (3) sins when we are suddenly tempted and taken unawares; (4) sins committed because the devil uses wounds and scars of past sins to excite the memory; (5) sins which are owing to a lack of practical experience or from ignorance of how to perform duties, for example, a man attempting to be munificent but who is prodigal; (6) sins which arise from unworthy motives and worldliness; (7) sins brought about by negligence and ignorance, for example, heedlessness, want of seriousness. All these are due to a lack of full consent on the part of the sinner or are involuntary. (*PPS* V, sermon 15)

Furthermore, Newman makes no distinction between eternal and temporal punishment due to sin. As long as the penalty is not paid in full, a sin is not entirely forgiven. No one can be certain that his sins have been forgiven. Speaking of serious men, he says, 'I will not lightly impute to any such man that he takes up the notion of his having been absolutely forgiven for the sins of his past life. Who is to forgive him? how is he to know it? No; I see not certainty for him. . . . his memory tells him that he has had sins upon his conscience; he has no warrant that they are not there still; and what has come, what is to come of them, what future consequences they imply, is unknown to him. . . . and looking on to the Day of Judgment, hope and fear both rise within him.' Nor can he be sure that 'God has forgiven it as to its eternal consequences.' Preaching the Anglican doctrine of an intermediate state instead of purgatory Newman could not speak of suffering for sin in an afterlife except in hell. All punishments for sin would seem to have to take place in this life, but at times Newman says we simply do not know. (PPS IV, sermon 8, pp. 123–26; IV, 3, p. 38)

So while sins of infirmity are blotted out by a life of faith and forgiveness by the presence of the Holy Spirit, transgressions, on the other hand, since they drive out the Holy Spirit can only be pardoned after a long course of continued acts of repentance. Since one never can be sure when this takes place, one has to live in fear and trembling, and practice continual repentance, prayer, penance, and patience.

Another limitation of Newman's doctrine of forgiveness as an Anglican is that he does not distinguish clearly between temptation and infirmities, nor between the tendency to sin, as a consequence of original sin (traditionally called 'concupiscence'), and sins that follow from it. (PPS V, 9, p. 120; VI, 1, p. 9) At times it seems that concupiscence is sin. (PPS V, 7, p. 90) One can understand, therefore, why one has constantly to be repenting of sins, because they are so frequent.[5]

As an Anglican Newman was not unaware of the doctrines of sacramental reconciliation, the distinction between mortal and venial sins and that between eternal and temporal punishment for sin, as well as the doctrine of purgatory, but he regarded them as Roman corruptions of the original revelation. (VM I, pp. 95ff.) In reexamining this contention in the light of the development of doctrine he was led to regard them as an example of logical development. From the earliest days of the Church it was admitted that baptism removes both actual and original sin. The question soon arose, however, about postbaptismal sins and how are they remitted, since baptism cannot be repeated. There gradually grew up a discipline of penance through which a sinner had to pass in order to be reconciled. In length and severity these penances varied with times and places. In reflecting upon these penances, Christians asked, were these punishments merely signs of contrition or were they in any sense satisfactions for sin? Newman concluded that there could be no doubt that the Fathers considered penances both as an expression of contrition and as a means of averting God's anger and punishment. Moreover, the prayers in the Eucharistic service for the faithful departed inculcated that sin not expiated on earth would receive punishment in the hereafter. 'Thus we see how, as times went on, the doctrine of purgatory was opened upon the apprehension of the Church, as a portion or form of Penance due for sins committed after Baptism.' (*Dev.*, pp. 383–99)

The difference which the acceptance of these doctrines of reconciliation made in Newman's approach to sin is easily discernable in the tone of Newman's Catholic as compared with his Anglican sermons. Instead of the vagueness about the forgiveness of sin, he explicitly recommends the sacrament of reconciliation and the hope and joy it brings: 'Whether you have sinned less or whether you have sinned more, He can make you as clean in His sight . . . as if you had never gone from Him. Gradually will He destroy your sinful habits, and at once will He restore you to His favour. Such is the power of the Sacrament of Penance, that, be your load of guilt heavier or be it lighter, it removes it, whatever it is.' Citing the cure of Naaman the Syrian from leprosy by the prophet Elijah, he comments: 'here, then, we have a representation not only what sin is, but of what God's grace is. It can undo the past, it can realize the hopeless. No sinner, ever so odious, but may become a Saint; no Saint, ever so exalted, but has been, or might have been, a sinner. Grace overcomes nature, and grace only overcomes it.' The tone in this sermon and in a similar one, 'The Religion of the Pharisee, the Religion of the world,' contrasts with that of Newman's sermons on sin in the *Parochial and Plain Sermons*. (*Mix.*, 3, pp. 56–57; *OS*, sermon 2)

Newman's *Parochial and Plain Sermons* have been criticized as harsh even to the extent of preaching a 'gospel of gloom,' devoid of joy. These criticisms have been effectively refuted,[6] but I think it has to be acknowledged that the vagueness about forgiveness of sin with a consequent overemphasis on the need of constant repentance, as well as Newman's confusion between the inclination to sin and sin itself have given some of the sermons on sin a gloomy cast indeed. On the other hand, in fairness to Newman it should be said that a number of contemporary readers of Volume 4 of the *Parochial Sermons,* which contains a number of the so-called gloomy sermons about sin, also found in the volume comfort and hope, and they wrote to tell him so. Presumably 'Peace and Joy amid Chastisement' and 'The State of Grace' are examples of these sermons. Nor does the aforesaid limitation undercut the value of his preaching about the horror of sin, the need for vigilance, the balancing of fear and love, the necessity of compunction and of grace—all of which Newman brought home to his hearers with great vividness and power. In an age which largely ignores the reality of sin and in which even Catholic priests complain that many of the faithful have lost the sense of sin, Newman's sermons offer a salutary antidote.

Notes

1. N to Miss Holmes, 21 February 1875, *LD* XXVII, p. 227; *GA*, p. 400.
2. N to Samuel Wilberforce, 10 March 1835, *LD* V, pp. 39–40.
3. In Newman's theology at the time of writing this sermon the Eucharist was not considered to be a sacrifice, which constitutes for a Catholic a serious limitation of Newman's doctrine of reparation.
4. Article Thirty-Five, 'Of the Sacraments,' of the Thirty-Nine Articles set down that only two sacraments were ordained by Christ: Baptism and the Lord's Supper. The others were not to be accounted for Sacraments of the Gospel, 'being such as have grown partly of the corrupt following of the Apostles, partly are states of life allowed in the Scriptures; but yet have not like nature of Sacraments with Baptism and the Lord's Supper, for that they have not any visible sign or ceremony ordained by God.' In *Tract* 90 Newman interpreted this to mean that Penance, though not instituted by Christ, was an 'outward sign of an inward grace.'

The Book of Common Prayer approved confessional absolution in some circumstances, for example, there was an alternate exhortation for the Communion Service which urged anyone troubled in conscience to approach God's minister for absolution before going to the table of the Lord's Supper. This was generally ignored by the clergy in Newman's day. In the service for visiting the sick the priest was directed to urge the sick person to make a special confession of his sins, and then to absolve him according to the formula set down, which was the one Newman used the first time he heard a confession upon request, 18 March 1838. (*AW,* pp. 214–15)

Newman revealed his hesitations about confession to Keble, 20 December 1842. (*Moz.* II, p. 405)

5. I am grateful to Robert A. Mitchell, S.J., from whom many years ago I first learned of the limitations and ambiguities in Newman's theology of sin.

6. Thomas Norris, 'Did Newman preach a Gospel of Gloom?' *The Irish Theological Quarterly,* 50 (1983–84), 198–211, in answer to A. B. Calkins, 'Newman's Gospel of Gloom,' *The Irish Theological Quarterly,* 49 (1982), 184–94.

Chapter Four

The World: Enemy and Sacrament

IF ONE IS to progress spiritually and to prepare for eternal life, to answer God's calls and invitations, one must become detached from the world. Again and again Newman sounded this note, but the meaning of the term 'world' took its precise nuance from the context in which he used it. Hence, it is imperative to understand accurately the various shades of meaning attached to the word.

It was through Thomas Scott that Newman was first introduced to these concepts, and he held fast to them. In a sermon, 'The World our Enemy' (*PPS* VII, sermon 3), Newman gave a detailed explanation of its various meanings. He first defines 'the world' as 'the present visible system of things, without taking into consideration whether it is good or bad. . . . it is the course of things which are carried on by human agency, with all its duties and pursuits,' and hence is not necessarily sinful. It is human society as it concretely operates, offering prizes for merit and exertion. Men rise above their fellows, gaining fame, honors, wealth, and power. 'The affairs of nations . . . the interchanges of production between country and country, are of this world.' It is the world for which the young are educated.

Nevertheless, though not sinful in itself, this state of affairs is likely to 'seduce our wayward hearts' from our true and eternal good. 'As the traveller on serious business may be tempted to linger, while he gazes on the beauty of the prospect which opens on his way, so this well-ordered and divinely-governed world, with all its blessings of sense and knowledge, may lead us to neglect those interests which endure when itself has passed away.' We see this world; the world of the spirit on the other hand is invisible and accessible only to faith, and inasmuch as sight has a stronger power over us than faith or belief, the human heart will tend to value sight over belief.

But there is another meaning to the word and in that sense the world is not only dangerous but sinful. It is this visible society of men as infected by sin from its birth, and the infection has spread throughout the entire system. 'Look into the history of the world. . . . Revolutions and changes without number, kingdoms rising and falling; and when without crime? States are established by God's ordinance, they have their existence in the necessity of man's nature; but when was one ever established, nay, or maintained, without war and bloodshed?' Thus, the affairs of nations are depraved by corrupt human nature. By reason of original sin, man collaborates with evil. 'Though we cannot keep from approving what is right in our conscience, yet we love and encourage what is wrong; so that when evil was once set up in the world, it was secured in its seat by the unwillingness with which our hearts relinquish it.' 'The course of human affairs viewed in its connexion with the principles, opinions, and practices which actually direct it'—this is what is meant by the sinful world. They are evil, and of these St John speaks: 'If any man love the world, the love of the Father is not in him. For all that is in the world, the lust of the flesh, and the lust of the eyes, and the pride of life, is not of the Father, but is of the world.'

Consequently, the world concretely existing is the enemy of the Christian soul, because its pursuits however good in themselves are likely to engross one, unless one is careful. Second, it is an enemy because 'in all its best pleasures, and noblest pursuits, the seeds of sin have been sown . . . so it is most difficult to enjoy the good without partaking of the evil also.'

It is this negative aspect of the world that Newman emphasizes in his sermons so as to warn his hearers of the dangers of 'worldliness.' So it is in the sermons, 'Temporal Advantages' and 'The Dangers of Riches.' In the former he gives reasons why wealth, fame, influence, and power are dangers to the Christian. Not only do they consume much time which might better be given to religious activity, but they tend to draw a man into an excessive love for them, withdrawing the heart from God. They then lead him to trust in them rather than in God. They become temptations not only against obedience but against faith. Temporal advantages have a tendency to make men self-confident and self-complacent. One of the examples cited is based upon his own early experience: 'When a man feels himself possessed of good abilities . . . or of powers of argument to discourse readily [on a subject], or of acuteness to detect fallacies in dispute . . . how will such a one be tempted to self-complacency and self-approbation.' (*PPS* VII, sermon 5)

The least satisfactory of these sermons is perhaps that entitled 'The Danger of Accomplishments,' in which Newman speaks of poetry, literary composition, painting, music, and the like as having the tendency to separate feeling from acting. They teach men to think, speak and be affected correctly, but they do not force him to practice what is right. Of course they don't nor are they meant to since they elicit contemplation rather than action. Musician and poet that he was, he certainly was not condemning the arts, but rather exposing the dangers involved in an immoderate use of them, an interpretation borne out by his example of novel reading which he directed to ladies of leisure who spent far too much time in this pastime. (*PPS* II, sermon 30)

In the sermon, 'The Dangers of Riches,' Newman explores the New Testament teaching which warns against not only the love of riches but their possession, because they can become a substitute for the One Object to which our supreme devotion is due. 'They are present; God is unseen.' Desiring and pursuing riches leads to substituting them as the aim and end of life rather than holiness and service of God. Moreover money gives a sense of power and tends to make one idolize oneself. Since what has been acquired with effort is not easily surrendered, wealthy men are commonly penurious and pinch-penny. When they give, they take plea-sure and pride in giving, and are unlikely to be liberal toward God, 'for religious offerings are an expenditure without sensible return.' This love of and pursuit of riches seemed to Newman the very characteristic of his age, and he had some strong statements to make about it. (*PPS* II, sermon 28; see also *PPS* VIII, 11, pp. 159–60).

How contrary such pursuits are to Christ's detachment from the world is evident from the Gospels. He scorned riches, worldly power, comfort, influence, fame, and honor. 'He came into the world, and speedily left the world, as if to teach us how little He himself, how little we His followers, have to do with the world.'

In exploring what Scripture sets down as the Christian, Newman affirms that his 'first great and obvious characteristic . . . is to be without

worldly ties or objects, to be living in this world, but not for this world.'
St Paul says, 'our conversation is in heaven,' or in other words, heaven is
our city. The essential mark of a Christian, whether he is rich or poor,
high or low, is that he has 'no aim of this world . . . whose thoughts and
aims have relation to the unseen, the future world,' and whose affections
are centered on Christ for whom he is constantly waiting. The very
definition of a Christian, says Newman, is 'one who looks for Christ, not
who looks for gain, or distinction, or power, or pleasure, or comfort.'
(*SD,* 19, pp. 278–79)

This separation from the world which marks the Christian character is
set forth in many texts of Scripture, for example, 'Love not the world,
neither the things there are in the world,' says St John, or 'Be not
conformed to this world, but be ye transformed by the renewing of your
mind,' says St Paul. (*SD,* 19, pp. 284–85)

The Mature Christian

It is natural, says Newman, for young people to look forward to life with
hopes and ambitions. They form schemes about what they will do when
they enter a profession. They dream of happiness, marriage, home, family, rising in the world, becoming famous, admired and respected, and
perhaps being rewarded with some high position. Such were James and
John when they wanted to be in the most honored positions in Christ's
kingdom. Generally these schemes are not sinful, except in a particular
case. But they are not what the mature Christian indulges in. A love of
worldly comforts and luxuries, vanity, conceit, boastfulness, are out of
place. To think that religious obedience consists in a few meagre observances of particular moral precepts easily complied with and to consider
this detachment from the world is immature. 'To put off idle hopes
of earthly good, to be sick of flattery and the world's praise, to see
the emptiness of temporal greatness, and to be watchful against self-
indulgence,—these are but the beginnings of religion; these are but the
preparation of heart, which religious earnestness implies; without a good
share of them, how can a Christian move a step?'

What then is Christian maturity? 'To read the events of life, as they
occur, by the interpretation which Scripture gives them, and . . . to do

it promptly,—to perform all our relative daily duties most watchfully,—
to check every evil thought, and bring the whole mind into captivity to
the law of Christ,—to be patient, cheerful, forgiving, meek, honest, and
true,—to persevere in this good work till death, making fresh and fresh
advances towards perfection—and after all, even to the end, to confess
ourselves unprofitable servants . . . these are some of the difficult realities of religious obedience, which we must pursue.' To break with the
world and to make religion our major concern is only to cease to be
children.

Is it not too severe to speak of such sacrifices at the beginning of true
Christian obedience? Newman replies: 'I have not said a word against
moderate and thankful enjoyment of this world's goods, *when* they actually come in our way; but against the wishing earnestly for them, seeking
them, and preferring them to God's righteousness. Further, I am not
excluding from the company of Christians all who cannot at once make up
their minds thus vigorously to reject the world, when its goods are
dangerous, inexpedient, or unsuitable; but excluding them from the
company of mature, manly Christians.' (*PPS* I, 26, pp. 339–47)

Christian Warfare

Insofar as the Christian does battle with the world as enemy, he becomes a
soldier of Christ, and his weapons are the weapons of the saints: self-
abasement rather than exaltation, humility rather than pride, poverty
rather than riches, forgiveness of enemies and doing good to them rather
than the satisfaction of revenge. Thus, 'the invisible powers of the heavens, truth, meekness, and righteousness are ever coming in upon the
earth, ever pouring in, gathering, thronging, warring, triumphing, under the guidance of Him who "is alive and was dead, and is alive for
evermore." The beloved disciple saw Him mounted on a white horse, and
going forth "conquering and to conquer." "And the armies which were in
heaven followed Him upon white horses, clothed in fine linen, white and
clean. And out of His mouth goeth a sharp sword, that with it He should
smite the nations, and He shall rule them with a rod of iron."' (Rev.
19:14, 15) (*PPS* VI, 22, p. 316)

The Christian is a living portion of that kingdom whose characteristic
is 'that the first should be last, and the last should be first,' and 'Whoso-

ever will be great among you, let him be your minister; and whosoever will be chief among you, let him be your servant; even as the Son of man came not to be ministered unto, but to minister.' Consequently, if one ministers to the humble and despised, feeds the hungry, assists the distressed, submits to insult, endures ingratitude, rendering good for evil, one is, 'as by a divine charm, getting power over the world and rising among the creatures. God has established this law. Thus He does His wonderful works. His instruments are poor and despised; the world hardly knows their names, or not at all.'

The Christian takes seriously Our Lord's injunction that at a wedding feast, one should take the lowest place, for he who humbles himself shall be exalted. And so the Christian cultivates here on earth all kinds of little humiliations, 'instead of loving display, putting ourselves forward, seeking to be noticed, being loud or eager in speech, and bent on having our own way, to be content, nay, to rejoice in being made little of, to perform what to the flesh are servile offices . . . to be patient under calumny; not to argue, not to judge, not to pronounce censures, unless a plain duty comes in; and all this because our Lord has said that such conduct is the very way to be exalted in His presence.' So with one's enemy, one seeks not revenge but to overcome him with love, to be kind and gentle, 'and while I cannot disguise from him that I know well where he stands, and where I, still this shall be with all peaceableness and purity of affection'— a hard duty, but one most blessed. (*PPS* VI, 22, pp. 319–23)

The World as Sacrament

At the same time Newman held a more positive view of the world, which has to be balanced against the former. It was based on the sacramental principle, namely, that God may be found symbolically in nature and in the supernatural system of revealed religion but only analogically. Newman imbibed it but only in an inchoate form from Keble's poems in the *Christian Year* and from Butler's *Analogy of Religion*. For example, Keble's poem on Septuagesima Sunday based on the text of St Paul to the Romans, I, 20:

The works of God, above below,
   Within us and around,

Are pages in that book, to show
How God Himself is found.

Only after reading the Alexandrian Fathers of the Church did this sacramental principle become explicit for Newman and thereafter consciously held.

There is an invisible world which the visible world subserves, directed by God's providence both general and personal. 'The visible world is the instrument, yet the veil, of the world invisible,—the veil, yet still partially the symbol and index: so that all that exists or happens visibly, conceals and yet suggests, and above all subserves, a system of persons, facts, and events beyond itself.' (*Ess.* II, p. 192) Both the Church's ritual, liturgy, and sacraments as well as the allegorical interpretation of Scripture require the exercise of a symbolical or sacramental mode of thinking. The allegorical interpretation of Scripture as developed by Clement and more especially by Origen recognized a double meaning in the record of scriptural events. Ceremonies, observances, and events were considered to have not only their own intrinsic meaning, but they were also recognized as signs, means, pledges of supernatural grace. All reality, the world, the Church, civil government, and man himself, are types and in different ways and at different times symbolic of a higher world which is its basis. Since, however, the sacraments of the Church are instrumental and symbolical by their very nature, while human and physical events seem to be more complete in themselves or even at times to run counter to the unseen system which they really subserve, symbolic knowledge makes demands upon faith. All reality, therefore, can be approached according to natural physical laws through methods unique and proper to the physical and historical sciences. This same reality can likewise be seen as symbolic, but the symbolical import is visible only to the eyes of faith. The knowledge which faith provides springs from principles interior to faith. These principles do not deny those of science but go beyond the latter and open vistas upon a higher reality.[1]

This sacramental view can be perceived, I think, in one of Newman's sermons, 'Doing Glory to God in Pursuits of the World.' In this sermon Newman is cautioning against an opposite tendency to attachment to this world. When one is detached from it, one is apt to undervalue this world's activities, to withdraw from active and social intercourse, to become lethargic, indifferent, or, in his Victorian terminology, 'to neglect one's duties in the world.' In those who do so, he says, 'we may be sure there is something wrong and unchristian, not in their thinking of the next world, but in their manner of thinking of it.' The true Christian, on the contrary, 'will see Christ revealed to his soul amid the ordinary actions of the day, as by a sort of sacrament. Thus he will take his worldly business as a gift from Him, and will love it as such.' In short, as on a well-balanced scale, he will seek an equilibrium between two truths: 'steadily to contemplate the world to come, yet to act in this.' (*PPS* VIII, sermon 11)

Newman's view of the world is an example of the traditional doctrine of the *coincidentia oppositorum*, the coming together of opposite truths or attitudes. The failure to recognize both sides of a truth led, Newman believed, to heresy. Heresy, he thought, was a partial view of truth, wrong not so much in what it says as in what it denies. So Newman, conscious of spiritual paradoxes, recognized that some persons suffering disappointment and disillusion with the world from that which they hoped would bring them good, learn to love God, 'not by baptismal grace, but by trial of the world; they seek the world, and they are driven by the world back to God. The world is blessed to them, in God's good providence, as an instrument of His grace transmuted from evil to good, as if a second sacrament, doing over again what was done in infancy, and then undone.' (*PPS* IV, 12, p. 186)

To keep from being seduced by the world and at the same time to find God in the events, Newman recommended an attitude of 'watching.' Newman explained what he meant by it: 'Do you know the feeling in matters of this life, of expecting a friend, expecting him to come, and he delays? Do you know what it is to be in unpleasant company, and to wish for the time to pass away, and the hour strike when you may be at liberty? Do you know what it is to be in anxiety lest something should happen which may happen or not, or to be in suspense about some important event, which makes your heart beat when you are reminded of it, and of which you think the first thing in the morning? Do you know what it is to have a friend in a distant country, to expect news of him, and to wonder from day to day what he is now doing, and whether he is well? . . . To watch for Christ is a feeling such as all these; as far as feelings of this world are fit to shadow out those of another.'

Such an attitude of watching for Christ involves a sacramental vision. 'He watches for Christ who has a sensitive, eager, apprehensive mind;

who is awake, alive, quick-sighted, zealous in seeking and honouring Him; who looks out for Him in all that happens, and who would not be surprised, who would not be over-agitated or overwhelmed, if he found he was coming at once.' Consequently, those who habitually watch for Christ never surrender their hearts to the world, even though they work in the world. They resist the temptation to substitute the temporal for the eternal. Those, on the contrary, who fail to watch for Christ, prefer this world to the next, make it their highest good, and never think that they will be separated from it. For them it has become an idol, and they, however morally good, are not really Christians. (PPS IV, 22, pp. 322ff.)

What are the characteristics of this waiting for Christ, which is founded on the virtue of hope? It is, Newman says, patient, subdued, tranquil, cheerful, and thoughtful. The evil in the world disturbs, but to attain to Christian hope the mind must have gone through a previous discipline which has already wrought it into a calm and quiet attitude of mind, in accordance with the saying of St Paul, 'patience worketh experience, and experience hope.' The prospect of future glory should fill the mind and strengthen it to submit with composure to the ills of life. Christian hope is not a passionate longing. The Christian is not thereby incapacitated for working in this world, or for making plans for the future; he goes about them with a merry heart in a subdued quiet way, watching at the same time for and meditating upon the promise given him, as Our Lady 'pondered these things in her heart.'

But the most important point that Newman makes is that hope is perfected by its *object,* which is of *common* interest to the *whole* Church. We should make light of our own private troubles and concentrate on those of the Church. Our troubles come and go, those of the Church go on from age to age: sinfulness, apostasy on the part of some of its members, quarrels, divisions into parties, breaches of unity. The day will come when these disorders will be set aright—perhaps in this world, certainly in heaven. This is one of the values of public prayers and the reception of the Eucharist, the sacrament of hope. (MS sermon no. 230)

Note

1. See V. F. Blehl, 'Newman, the Fathers, and Education,' *Thought,* 45 (Summer 1970), 196–212, especially pp. 210–12, for a thorough discussion of these ideas.

II Christ and the Holy Spirit

Chapter Five

Christ the Incarnate Savior

ALIENATED from God by original and personal sin, man cannot achieve by his own efforts the end for which he was created. In the divine plan for man's redemption he can do so only through Christ, the incarnate Son of God. The Evangelical preaching of Christ was largely restricted to the doctrine of his atonement, which was regarded as the central doctrine of Christianity and the instrument of conversion to it. Newman, however, came to believe that the preaching of the atonement was not the ordinary way irreligious men were converted to Christ. The atonement, he said, was 'an object for devotion, not for conversion.' It was a mystery, and therefore to be reverenced as such. In a sermon with reference to the contemporary preaching of the Evangelicals, he remarked, 'It is very much the fashion at present to regard the Saviour of the world in an irreverent and unreal way—as a mere idea or vision; to speak of Him so narrowly and unfruitfully as if we only knew His name. . . . And till we learn . . . to leave off vague statements about His love, His willingness to receive the sinner, His imparting repentance and spiritual aid and the like, and view Him in His particular and actual works, set before us in Scripture, surely we have not derived from the Gospels that very benefit which they are intended to convey.' (*PPS* III, 10, pp. 130–31)[1]

Newman's strategy in preaching was different. 'When men are to be exhorted to newness of life, the true Object to be put before them, as I conceive, is "Jesus Christ, the same yesterday, today, and for ever"; the true Gospel preaching is to enlarge, as they can bear it, on the Person, natures, attributes, offices, and work of Him who once regenerated them, and is now ready to pardon; to dwell upon His recorded words and deeds on earth; to declare reverently and adoringly His mysterious greatness as

the Only-begotten Son, One with the Father, yet distinct from Him, yet
not apart from Him; eternal, yet begotten; a Son, yet as if a servant; and
to combine and to contrast His attributes and relations to us as God and
man, as our Mediator, Saviour, Sanctifier, and Judge. The true preaching
of the Gospel is to preach Christ.' (*Jfc.*, p. 325; *PPS* III, 11, p. 148; II,
sermon 15)[2]

The Incarnation

Newman came to look upon the incarnation 'as the great doctrine of the
Gospel.' Speaking of Christianity as 'eminently an objective religion,
which for the most part tells us of persons and facts in simple words, and
leaves that announcement to produce its effect on such hearts as are
prepared to receive it,' Newman cited 'the revealed doctrine of the Incarnation,' which 'exerted a stronger and broader influence on Christians, as
they more and more apprehended and mastered its meaning and its
bearings.' The incarnation is announced in Scripture, he said, in the
simple words 'The Word was made flesh, and dwelt among us.' These
words which convey everything sufficed for the early Christians until
misconceptions arose and then they had to be explained, so that creeds are
an additional help in presenting the reality of what we are told in Scripture. These statements, for example, in the Te Deum and the Athanasian
Creed, are not cold bare formal propositions and abstractions conveying
mere notions. They are 'hymns of praise and thanksgiving; they give
glory to God as revealed in the Gospel, just as David's Psalms magnify
His attributes as displayed in nature, His wonderful works in the creation
of the world, and His mercies towards the house of Israel.' Hence, they
are especially suited to divine worship inasmuch as they kindle religious
affections.(*Diff.* II, p. 86; *PPS* II, 3, pp. 27–28)[3]
 Preaching on the text, 'The Word was made flesh, and dwelt among
us,' Newman gave a short explanation of the meaning of the doctrine of
the incarnation. The Word, the Only-begotten Son of God before all
worlds were created, was in existence, in the bosom of the Eternal Father,
God from God, and light from light, 'supremely blessed in knowing and
being known of Him, and receiving all divine perfections from Him, yet
ever One with Him who begat Him.' To the question why is He called

the Word, Newman answered, 'If we may dare conjecture, He is called the Word of God, as mediating between the Father and all creatures, bringing them into being, fashioning them, giving the world its laws, imparting reason and conscience to creatures of a higher order, and revealing to them in due season the knowledge of God's will.'

The incarnation is another and perhaps more remarkable manifestation of God's love for man. That love had first been shown in the creation of man, but when Adam fell and as a result he and his descendants were alienated from God, 'that unsearchable Love, which showed itself in our original creation . . . brought Him down again from His Father's bosom to do His will, and repair the evil which sin had caused. And with a wonderful condescension He . . . humbled Himself; suffering all the infirmities of our nature in the likeness of sinful flesh, all but a sinner,— pure from all sin, yet subjected to all temptation,—and at length becoming obedient unto death, even the death of the cross.' He came therefore as the Son of Man, but not as the son of sinful Adam. He had no earthly father, but was born of the Virgin Mary, who thus became the Mother of God. He was truly God and Man, One Person—not two, but One Christ. Newman includes in this account of the incarnation the subsequent events, if one can call them that, of Christ's history, namely, that He 'preached the Gospel, chose His Apostles, suffered on the cross, died, and was buried, rose again and ascended on high, there to reign till the day when He comes again to judge the world. This is the All-gracious Mystery of the Incarnation, good to look into, good to adore; according to the saying in the text, "The word was made flesh,—and dwelt among us."'

Newman then tried to make the doctrine more distinct by differentiating it from other manifestations of God, as an Angel in the Old Testament, for example, or by participation in the divine Nature by reason of a divine indwelling. But neither of these involves the union of a human nature, body and soul, with a divine nature, and such is the incarnation. Even in death Christ's human nature was not separated from the divine nature but conjoined to it. And so Newman concluded the sermon with the exhortation, 'let us praise and bless Him in the Church below, whom Angels in heaven see and adore. Let us bless Him for His surpassing loving-kindness in taking upon Him our infirmities to redeem us, when He dwelt in the innermost love of the everlasting Father, in the glory which He had with Him before the world was.' (*PPS* II, sermon 3)

Christ the Son of God

Another important aspect of Newman's view of the incarnation is clearly brought out in one of his sermons, 'Christ the Son of God made Man.' (*PPS* VI, sermon 5) Here he insists that while Christ is God, He is God because He is the *Son* of God. Only thus, Newman claims, is one true to what Scripture teaches: 'As the Father hath life in Himself, so hath He given to the Son to have life in Himself'; 'The Father hath not left Me alone'; 'My Father worketh hitherto, and I work'; 'I am in the Father, and the Father in Me.' Though these passages can be understood to refer to Our Lord's human nature, Newman felt that to confine them to this interpretation ran the risk of viewing Christ as two separate beings, not as one Person; or, again, of gradually forgetting and explaining away the doctrine of His divinity altogether. Such passages 'would seem to speak neither of Christ's human nature, nor of the divine, solely, but of both together, that is, of Him who being the Son of God is also man. . . . [He] was in the Father and the Father in Him, not only from eternity but in time.'

Hence, it is neither the Father nor the Holy Spirit who became man, 'but the Son of the Father, God the Son, God from God, and Light from Light, who came down upon earth, and who thus, though graciously taking on Him a new nature, remained as He had been from everlasting, the *Son* of the Father, and spoke and acted towards the Father as a Son.' Moreover, it was to His Eternal Person that His human nature was so intimately conjoined, and this 'absolutely and entirely belonging to Him as really as His justice, truth, or power; so that it would be as unmeaning to speak of dividing one of His attributes from Him as to separate from Him His manhood.' This perfect unity consists, however, not in a unity of *nature,* but in a unity of *Person.* Christ's manhood 'never subsisted except as belonging to His divinity; it has no subsistence in itself.'

When Newman treats of any action, deed, or work of Christ, he never loses sight of the fact that this is an act of the Son of God, and he inserts some statement to this effect. For example, in the sermon, 'The Incarnate Son, a Sufferer and Sacrifice,' he traces the stages of Christ's passion but pauses to remind his hearers who it is that is suffering the indignities. 'Now I bid you consider that that Face, so ruthlessly smitten, was the Face of God Himself; the Brows bloody with the thorns, the sacred Body exposed to view and lacerated with the scourge, the Hands nailed to the Cross, and, afterwards, the Side pierced with a spear; it was the Blood, and the sacred Flesh, and the Hands, and the Temples, and the Side, and the Feet of God Himself, which the frenzied multitude then gazed upon. This is so fearful a thought, that . . . while we think of it, we must pray God to temper it to us, and to give us the strength to think of it rightly, lest it be too much for us.' (*PPS* VI, 6, p. 74) He later owned that he loved to dwell on Christ as the Only-begotten Word, nor did he think it any forgetfulness of Christ's humanity to contemplate His Eternal Person, since it is the very idea that He is God which gives meaning to His sufferings. 'What is to me a man, and nothing more, in agony, or scourged or crucified? . . . But here I see One . . . stretched upon the Cross, and He is God.' (*Mix.,* 15, pp. 320–21)

This orientation accounts for Newman's keen realization of the nature of Christ's humiliation and condescension in becoming incarnate— condescension in the sense of 'unmerited kindness.' Only one who under- stands in some way, however limited, the eternity, infinity, and omnipo- tence of the Divine Person can appreciate what this was. Bishop Clifford in his homily at Newman's funeral mass affirmed that Newman's descrip- tions of the divine attributes are some of the most beautiful and powerful portions of his writings. Some of these would be 'The Mystery of Divine Condescension' (*Mix.,* sermon 14), 'The Infinitude of the Divine Attri- butes' (*Mix.,* sermon 15), and 'Omnipotence in Bonds' (*OS,* sermon 6). In the first of these by the use of analogies Newman conveys a sense of what it means to live an eternity without beginning, by Himself, and not to be weary of the solitude. Unlike men who can't bear to be alone for any length of time, or prisoners in solitary confinement who can verge on madness, it is incomprehensible how God lived forever from eternity, never wearying of His own infinity, completely happy and joyous, so much so that the creation of a universe and a world of men added nothing to His happiness.

In the sermon 'Omnipotence in Bonds,' Newman discourses for four and a half pages on the mystery of omnipotence, tracing it back to the notion of eternity. 'For ages innumerable, for infinite periods, long and long before any creature existed, He was. When there was no creature to exercise His power upon, He was omnipotent. . . . He can decree and bring to pass, He can direct, control, and resolve, absolutely according to

His will. He could create this vast material world, with all its illimitable spaces, in a moment. All its overwhelming multiplicity of laws, and complexity of formations, and intricacy of contrivances, both to originate and to accomplish, is with Him but the work of a moment. He could destroy it all in all its parts in a moment; in the same one moment He could create another universe instead of it, indefinitely more vast, more beautiful, more marvellous, and indefinitely unlike that universe He was annihilating. He could bring into existence and destroy an infinite series of such universes, each in succession more perfect than that which immediately preceded it.' (OS, 6, pp. 77–78)

Only by an appreciation of God's attributes—and the foregoing excerpts hardly do justice to Newman's imaginative grasp of them—can our finite minds realize in a poor and limited way the depths of the Son's humiliation, His emptying Himself, in the incarnation especially in His death on the cross. 'Omnipotence became an abject [sic]; the Life became a leper; the first and only Fair came down to us with an "inglorious visage," and an "unsightly form," bleeding and . . . ghastly, lifted up in nakedness and stretched out in dislocation before the eyes of sinners.' But He has done more. He had made it the symbol of His religion and when He comes again that sign of the Son of Man will be seen in Heaven. When He takes His seat in judgment, 'the same glorious marks will be seen by all the world in His Hands, Feet, and Side.' (Mix., 15, pp. 315–17)

The Form of a Servant

In what did the humiliation of the Son of God consist, as spoken of in the text in Hebrews that 'though He were a Son, yet learned He obedience by the things which He suffered'? (Heb. 5:7, 8) Newman explains by affirming that obedience more properly belongs to a servant than to a son. 'In His eternal union with the Father there was no distinction of wills and work between Him and His Father,' but in becoming man He took on a separate will and a separate work. Consequently, though He was a Son, yet in his manhood He had experience of *obedience.* Moreover, He learned it amid suffering and temptation.

The Word did not descend upon a preexisting man but took to Himself man's nature in all its completeness. Thus, He made the created essence 'the instrument' of His humiliation. 'He was born of the Virgin Mary, He had a natural fear of danger, a natural shrinking from pain,' and so He prayed that the cup of suffering might pass from Him. In short, 'that Eternal Mind, which, till then, had thought and acted as God, began to think and act as a man, with all man's faculties, affections, and imperfections, sin excepted. Before He came on earth He was infinitely above joy and grief, fear and anger, pain and heaviness; but afterwards all these properties and many more were His as fully as they are ours. . . . Before He came on earth, He could not be tempted of evil; but afterwards He had a man's heart, a man's tears, and a man's wants and infirmities.'

What struck Newman in the doctrine of the incarnation was this mystery of God's humiliation or lowering Himself to a creaturely status, to temptation, and to suffering. He thought the incarnation more overwhelming than the mystery of the Trinity, which when we consider it we at once see it is beyond our comprehension, but 'the mystery of the Incarnation relates to subjects more on the level with our reason; it lies not only in the manner how God and man is one in Christ, but in the very fact that so it is.' Hence, the mystery lies as much in what we think we know, as in what we do not know.

Newman cites some examples to illustrate what he means. Why was Christ tempted when our redemption is ascribed to His death, not to it? How came Satan to have such power over Him as to be able to transport Him from place to place? Again, the mystery of the connection of His temptation with the descent of the Holy Spirit upon Him at His baptism. '*Immediately* the Spirit *driveth* Him into the wilderness.' Such questions make us realize how little we know, though what we do know should be enlarged upon, and this is what Newman attempted to do in the sermon, 'The Humiliation of the Eternal Son,' and others. To the objection that these explanations were too abstract, speculative, and unprofitable, he replied, 'What do we gain from words, however correct and abundant, if they end in themselves, instead of lighting up the image of the Incarnate Son in our hearts?' (*PPS* III, sermon 12)

The Atoning Sacrifice

While stressing Christ's divinity Newman did not lose sight of the fact that Christ suffered in His humanity, and that His sufferings were undergone 'voluntarily, "not grudgingly or of necessity," but done cheerfully doing God's will.' He was not merely passive in His sufferings, but accounted it 'as if a great occasion for a noble and severe surrender of Himself to His Father's will.' The effect of pain is to turn one inwards and become selfish, but Christ's sufferings were borne without the thought of self, rather with love toward His Father and toward men. 'Even when He seemed to be thinking of Himself, and said, "I thirst," He really was regarding the words of prophecy, and was bent on vindicating, to the very letter, the divine announcements concerning Him. . . . His mind was stayed upon His Father's sovereign will and infinite perfections, yet could pass, without effort, to the claim of filial duty, or the need of an individual sinner. Six out of His seven last words were words of faith and love.' (*PPS* III, 11, pp. 149–50)

The result of the Son's taking upon Himself a human nature in which He suffered and died in obedience to the will of the Father was that He died as an 'Atoning Sacrifice,' whose result was the reconciliation of man to God, the expiation of our sins, and our new creation in holiness. 'Human nature, fallen and corrupt, was under the wrath of God, and it was impossible that it should be restored to His favour till it had expiated its sin by suffering. Why this was necessary, we do not know.' God could have pardoned mankind without becoming man and without exacting expiation. The Son of God, however, took upon Himself a sinless nature—for sinlessness was an essential of the atoning act—that in Him it might do what it could not do of itself. 'In Him our sinful nature died and rose again. . . . It became a Divine leaven of holiness for the new birth and spiritual life of as many as should receive it. And thus, as the Apostle says, "if one died for all, then did *all* die"; "our old man is crucified *in Him,* that the *body* of sin might be destroyed"; and "together" with Christ "when we were dead in sins, hath He quickened us, and raised us up together, and made us sit together in heavenly places in Christ Jesus."' And thereby we become members of His body. (*PPS* VI, sermon 6)

The doctrine of Christ's atonement is clearly set forth in Scripture. Christ Himself alluded to His coming sacrifice when He spoke of laying down His life for the sheep (John 10), of drawing all men to Himself when lifted up on the cross, of giving His life as a ransom for many (Matt. 20), and at the Last Supper when He announced that His blood would be shed for the remission of sin. (Matt. 22) Likewise in the Epistles is there reference to His giving Himself up for us, for example, Eph. 5 and Col. 1. 'God has made Him to be sin that we might be made the righteousness of God in Him' (2 Cor. 5), and in Rom. 3:25–26, 'Being justified freely by His grace through the redemption that is in Christ Jesus—whom God hath set forth to be a propitiation . . . to declare His righteousness for the remission of sins that are past.' So also St John affirms, 'He is the propitiation for our sins, He loved us and washed us from our sins in His blood' (Rev. 1), and 'He hath redeemed us to God by His blood.' (Rev. 5) Finally St Peter writes, 'He carried our sins in His body to the cross. It is by His wounds you have been healed.' (1 Pet. 2)

Christ's sinlessness is often mentioned in Scripture, for it was essential, Newman affirmed, for this office of atonement, man's sinfulness rendering him unable to offer such a reparation. St Peter, for example, says, 'Ye are redeemed with the precious blood of Christ, as of a lamb without blemish and without spot.' (1 Pet. 1) Newman thought it important to dwell upon Christ's sinlessness, for unless we have it before our eyes, we cannot feel toward Christ both due gratitude and due awe. Many experience joy at the news of their redemption; few recognize, he felt, that it should also inspire fear, in the sense of awe. This is another example of the *coincidentia oppositorum,* or the coming together of opposite attitudes or virtues. 'The thought of the Immaculate Lamb of God is a strong ground of trust, in that He is immaculate—and for the reason of deep awe also.' (MS sermon no. 533)

Newman disagreed with the attempts of the Evangelicals to regard the atonement as a manifestation of God's justice. Christ died, says Newman, 'not in order to exert a peremptory claim on the divine justice, if I may so speak,—as if He were bargaining in the market-place, or pursuing a plea in a court of law; but in a more loving, generous munificent way, did He shed that blood . . . in accordance with His Father's will, who, for wise reasons unrevealed, exacted it as the condition of their pardon.' Furthermore, one drop of His blood would have been sufficient to satisfy for our sins, but He emptied Himself. 'This is what the Apostle intimates in saying that we are "bought with a *great* price"; and the prophet, while he declares that "with the Lord there is mercy, and with Him a *copious*" or "*plenteous* redemption."' It was as if He delighted in having to suffer. 'It is, if we may use human language, a prodigality of charity or that heroic love of toil and hardship, which is poorly shadowed out in the romantic defenders of the innocent or the oppressed . . . who have gone about the earth, nobly exposing themselves to peril for any one who asked their aid.' It was 'royal munificence' of an infinite kind. (*Mix.*, 15, pp. 307–11)

Christ the Mediator

Christ having atoned for the sins of men is a mediator between God and man 'as being a *means of blessings* from God to man—the channel through which divine pardon, knowledge, strength, holiness and happiness are conveyed to us. We are blest *for His* sake, as His subjects, as members of His mediatorial Kingdom.' Mediation is not something uncommon in man's experience. In God's providence over society, men are mediators of goods to others. None of the ordinary blessings of the day, whether home, house, food, medicine come directly from God but through the instrumentality of other men. In the Old Testament there were mediators between God and man, such as Moses, Joshua, Samuel, David, and others. There were also other extraordinary mediators, sometimes called *angels,* or messengers. The Church is a mediator of supernatural blessings.

Christ's mediatorship differs from all others whether natural or supernatural in that 'Christ has a *power* and *a claim* with God which others have not.' His mediation is meritorious. Moreover, since God appointed him to this office, His mediation with the Father is certain, 'God has chosen us *in* Him—. . . having fore-appointed us to be adopted as His children *through Jesus Christ.*' (Eph. 1) Scripture likewise speaks of our *redemption,* meaning literally 'a buying back'—a purchasing, that is, of a sinful race from misery into a kingdom of grace and hope, the price being His life. (MS sermon no. 178)

In conclusion, 'Christ must be the glory of God shining in each of our hearts'—turning us by His Spirit from darkness, to light—from the love of sin to holiness—from disobedience to God to a life of practical piety, of faith, and works of righteousness. (MS sermon no. 176)

Notes

1. See also Newman's citation of the sermons of Chalmers as an example of how the emphasis on the atonement 'excites the feelings rather than mends the

Heart.' (*KC*, p. 206; *PPS* VI, 7, p. 90; *LD* XXX, pp. 181, 188, 204) Newman proposed the incarnation as the central truth of Christianity. (*Dev.*, pp. 324–26)

2. The source of Newman's doctrine on Christ was first the Scriptures. Jaak Seynaeve concluded his study of Newman and the Scriptures with the assertion that for Newman, 'Christ Himself . . . is the unifying principle par excellence in the whole of the Bible narrative, whether it be the historical Christ with regard to both Old and New Testaments, or the eschatological Christ in these last times. It is one and the same Christ; typified in the Old, God incarnate in the New, He will be our heavenly reward after His second coming.' (Jaak Seynaeve, *Cardinal Newman's Doctrine on Holy Scripture according to his published works and previously unedited manuscripts,* Louvain and Oxford 1953, p. 305) There was also, however, another influence: that of the Fathers of the Church, especially St Athanasius. The influence of the Fathers of the Church and particularly that of St Athanasius has been shown in detail in the comprehensive work on Newman's 'Christology' by Roderick Strange, *Newman and the Gospel of Christ,* Oxford 1981.

3. See also Newman's remarks in the *Grammar of Assent* that the Athanasian Creed 'is not a mere collection of notions. . . . It is a psalm or hymn of praise. . . . It appeals to the imagination quite as much as to the intellect.' (*GA,* p. 133)

Chapter Six

The Indwelling Spirit of Christ

The Risen Christ

Long before twentieth-century liturgists and theologians began to stress
that the sacrifice of Christ on the cross cannot be separated from His
resurrection, that the latter was an integral part of the entire redemptive
action of Christ, Newman grasped this clearly and preached it to his
parishioners. The resurrection was part of what he called the 'gracious
economy' of the incarnation. This redemption was not merely a one-time
act on the cross; it created an entire new order of being in which those
who believe would be introduced. But belief would be precisely belief in
Christ risen from the dead.

Christ's resurrection was a manifestation of His glory. It gave testi-
mony to His divine origin. 'He was *declared* to be the Son of God with
power, according to the Spirit of Holiness'; that is, 'His essential God-
head.' When he rose from the dead 'the Divine essence streamed forth (so
to say) on every side, and environed His Manhood, as a cloud of glory.' So
transfigured was His Sacred Body 'that He who had deigned to be born of
a woman, and to hang upon the cross, had a subtle virtue in Him, like a
spirit, to pass through the closed doors to His assembled followers. . . .
He manifested Himself to them in this exalted state.' (PPS II, 13, pp.
141–43)

Nevertheless, Christ did not make a public display of His glory to all
the people or to His enemies, but only 'unto witnesses chosen before of
God.' Newman assigned as the reason for this that it 'was the most
effectual means of propagating His religion through the world.' He revealed Himself to a select few whom He trained and stamped upon their
mind the thought and image of Him 'as the one master-spring of their
whole course of life for the future.' In so doing He was 'but acting

according to the general course of His providence,' for every great change, according to Newman's habitual belief, 'is effected by the few, not by the many; by the resolute, undaunted, zealous few.' No less startling is Newman's statement that the real object of His rising again was 'the propagation of His Gospel through the world by *means* of His own intimate friends and followers.' (*PPS* I, sermon 22)

Moreover, no sharp division can be made between Christ's resurrection and His ascension. The latter was the closing, as it were, of 'the economy of His Incarnation.' Christ, the holy One, was ordained not only to die a redemptive death, but to be by it, 'the beginning' of a new 'creation' unto holiness, in our sinful race; to refashion soul and body after His own likeness, that they might be 'raised together, and sit together in heavenly places in Christ Jesus.' Christ communicates life to each one by means of His holy and incorrupt nature which He assumed for our redemption. How He does this, we do not know, but we know that it is a real communication, even though unseen. And so St Paul says that 'the last Adam was made' not merely 'a living soul,' but a 'quickening' or life-giving 'Spirit,' as being 'the Lord from Heaven.'

It is not only by reason of His divine nature that Christ is present to us, but 'personally, as the Christ, as God and man; not present with us locally and sensibly, but still really, in our hearts and to our faith.' (*PPS* VI, 10, pp. 126, 133) In explaining the teaching of St Athanasius on this union with Christ, Newman later wrote, 'Our Lord, by becoming man, has found a way whereby to sanctify that nature of which His own manhood is the pattern specimen. He inhabits us personally, and this inhabitation is effected by the channels of the Sacraments. . . . By this indwelling our Lord is the immediate *archē* [source, or first principle] of spiritual life to each of His elect individually.' He then quotes St Athanasius's words 'because of our relationship to His Body we too have become God's temple, and in consequence are made God's sons.' (*Ath.* II, pp. 193–95)

The Risen Christ and the Holy Spirit

At various times Newman distinguished between Christ's redemption and the communication of the results of that redemption to men. 'The

Atonement for sin took place during His own Mission, and He was the Chief Agent; the application of that Atonement takes place during the mission of His Spirit, who accordingly is the Agent of it.' (*Jfc.*, p. 204) To show the intimate connection between Christ and the Holy Spirit, the Holy Spirit is referred to as the Spirit of Christ. As St Paul says, 'God hath sent forth the Spirit of His Son into your hearts.' The communication of Christ's sacrifice on the cross 'is not the communication of that Body and Blood such as it was when offered upon the Cross, but, in a higher, glorified, and spiritual state. . . . the crucified Man, the Divine Son, comes again to us in His Spirit. . . . He came first in the flesh; He has come the second time in the Spirit.' The presence of Christ in the soul is achieved through the presence of the Holy Spirit. The Spirit 'comes that Christ may come in His coming. Through the Holy Ghost we have communion with the Father and Son.' (*PPS* VI, 10, p. 126)

Newman also noted that there seemed to be a mysterious connection between Christ's ascension and His returning in the Person of His Spirit. 'He said that unless He went, His Spirit would not come to us; as though His ascending and the Spirit's descending, if not the same act, yet were very closely connected, and admitted of being spoken of as the same.' Moreover the 'Divine Life which raised Him, flowed over, and availed unto our rising again from sin and condemnation. It wrought a change in His Sacred Manhood, which became spiritual, without His ceasing to be man, and was in a wonderful way imparted to us as a new-creating, transforming Power in our hearts. Consequently God the Son and God the Holy Spirit have so acted together in their separate Persons that it is difficult at times to discriminate what belongs to each respectively. Christ rises by His own power, yet the Holy Spirit is said to raise Him.' (*Jfc.*, pp. 205–9) The new life imparted to the Christian is a participation or sharing in the risen and glorified Christ who, through the Spirit makes God present to him. (*Jfc.*, pp. 205–9, 218–19)

Effects of the Indwelling of the Holy Spirit

In a sermon, 'The Indwelling of the Spirit' Newman affirmed that the Holy Spirit dwells in the body and soul of a Christian, as in a temple. 'All knowing and omnipresent He is able to search all our thoughts, and penetrate into every motive of the heart.' He pervades us like light in a room or a perfume in a robe. The effects of this indwelling are momentous. 'Such an inhabitation brings the Christian into a state altogether new and marvellous, far above the possession of mere gifts, exalts him inconceivably in the scale of beings, and gives him a place and an office which he had not before. In St Peter's forcible language, he becomes a "partaker of the Divine Nature," and has "power" or authority, as St John says, "to become the son of God."' This new birth through the entrance of the Holy Spirit is called regeneration. 'All guilt and pollution are burned away as by fire, the devil is driven out, sin, original and actual, is forgiven, and the whole man is consecrated to God.' (*PPS* II, 19, p. 222)

The indwelling of the Holy Spirit renders one holy before God and enables the soul to perform works of holiness, in biblical terminology, to be righteous. To be righteous, Newman explains, 'is to act up to the Law, whatever the Law be, and thereby to be acceptable to the one who gave it.' Such was Adam in Paradise; he was righteous, but in sinning, he forfeited the presence of the Holy Spirit. Hence, he could no longer fulfill the law; he had lost righteousness, knowing God's law but being unable to fulfill it.

Through the prophets God promised to restore this. '*I will put My Law in their inward parts,* and write it in their hearts,' says Jeremiah, and Ezekiel describes the great gift of the Gospel, '*A new heart* also will I give you, and a *new spirit* will I put within you; and I will put *My Spirit* within you, and *cause you* to walk in My statutes, and ye shall keep my Judgments and do them.' This is also called in the prophets 'the robe of righteousness.' Holy men are called righteous before God, or in God's sight. To be righteous before God is to bear His scrutiny that one is really righteous. Now St Paul teaches that this righteousness is conferred by the Holy Spirit, who justifies us and makes us acceptable in God's sight. No work of ours is perfect, and therefore viewed in its imperfection, cannot justify. 'But when I speak of our righteousness I speak of the work of the Spirit, and this work, though imperfect, considered as ours, is perfect as far as it comes from Him. Our works, done in the Spirit of Christ, have a justifying *principle* in them, and that is the presence of the All-holy Spirit. His influences are infinitely pleasing to God, and able to overcome in His sight all our own infirmities and demerits.'

It is the presence of the Holy Spirit, therefore, which makes the soul holy, which sanctifies all our acts and renders our obedience to God acceptable and holy in His sight. 'All solemn, reverent, thankful, and devoted feelings, all that is noble, all that is choice in the regenerate soul, all that is self-denying in conduct, and zealous in action, is drawn forth and offered up by the Spirit as a living sacrifice to the Son of God.' By such good actions the soul grows in holiness until it is perfected in heaven, when faith yields to sight. (*PPS* V, sermon 11)

Moreover, the Holy Spirit reveals to us the God of mercies and tells us to recognize and adore Him as our Father. The Spirit impresses on us the image of the Heavenly Father, lost through Adam, and gives back a portion of that freedom that was lost, of uprightness and innocence, which Adam once had. He unites and connects all Christians in one family, that is everywhere holy and eternal, and enables the individual soul to mount up to the Father, to cry to Him continually, according to St Paul's assertion, 'Ye have received the Spirit of adoption, whereby we cry, "Abba, Father."' He who has sent the Spirit to dwell in us habitually has moreover given us a form of prayer whereby we may address the Father, namely, the Lord's Prayer. (*PPS* II, sermon 19)

The Holy Spirit is also 'the earnest of our inheritance,' and 'the seal and earnest of an unseen Saviour.' (Eph. 1:4; 2 Cor. 1:22; 5:5) An earnest is something given in advance of what is one day to be given in full. 'He shall quicken even your mortal bodies by His Spirit that dwelleth in you.' The real body of the regenerated soul is not only material, but spiritual, of which the seed is now deposited within us. 'As Adam diffused death, so the life-giving Spirit is the seed and principle of spiritual bodies to all who are His.' One of the corollaries of this doctrine is that the body must be treated with reverence because it is sanctified. This was also the reason for the veneration of the relics of the saints; and 'the religious veneration in which even the living have sometimes been held, who, being saintly, were distinguished by miraculous gifts.' (*Jfc.*, pp. 211–12; *PPS* II, 19, pp. 220–21; *Dev.*, p. 400)

The fruits of the Spirit, according to Galatians 5:22–23, are 'love, joy, peace, long-suffering, gentleness, goodness, faith, meekness, temperance.' Newman points out that the word *Spirit* is used by St Paul to denote that special character which the Holy Spirit has promised to form in the hearts of Christians, in whom He dwells. The most important of these is the grace of love. It is described with its accompanying graces in the epistle. For example, 'let love be without dissimulation . . . be kindly affectioned one to another with brotherly love; in honor preferring one another . . . distributing to the necessity of saints—given to hospitality—bless them which persecute you: bless and curse not—rejoice with them that do rejoice, and weep with them that weep— . . . mind not high things but condescend to men of low estate— . . . avenge not yourselves . . . be not overcome of evil, but overcome evil with good.' (Rom. 12) Again, 'Let us not be desirous of vainglory, provoking one another, envying one another.' (Gal. 5) 'Bear ye one another's burdens and so fulfill the lae of Christ.' (Gal. 6) 'Let all bitterness and wrath and anger and clamour and evil-speaking be put away from you, with all malice— and be ye kind one to another, tender-hearted, forgiving one another, even as God for Christ's sake hath forgiven you.' (Eph. 4) St Paul in the 13th chapter of 1 Corinthians, and St James in the third chapter of his epistle have given descriptions of this spirit of love.

Newman in one sermon concentrates on this spirit of love as an abiding habit through the day that influences one's conduct in all one's business and family relations. It forces one's attention on the small and ordinary matters that occupy us, making one amiable, kind, cheerful, considerate and affectionate as a friend, companion, and associate. 'Indeed,' remarks Newman, 'many of the precepts of the Apostles, if taken by themselves, might even stand for the mere rules for good behaviour in the intercourse of life rather than strict religious directions, so active and penetrating is Christian love, when it governs a man, so practical and condescending.' It differs, as Newman showed in detail in the 8th Discourse of the 'Discourses on University Education,' in the *Idea of a University,* in flowing from a *religious* principle and motive.

The Holy Spirit creates this loving disposition in the heart of the Christian after the pattern of Christ, whose incarnation and whole life was 'one of condescending assiduous love.' His miracles of compassion wrought on the sick, the poor, the maimed, and the blind; his invitations and patient instruction of publicans and sinners; his solicitude for his apostles; his love and care of children and 'the little ones'—all set a pattern for the Christian. 'Whosoever shall give to drink unto one of these little ones a cup of cold water only in the name of a disciple, verily I say unto you, he in no wise loses His reward.' Almsgiving is made the condition of admission into His kingdom of glory: 'In as much as ye have done it unto one of the least of these My brethren, ye have done it unto Me.'

The Holy Spirit in the Church

Newman's thought and spirituality might be termed 'personal' yet such a descriptive label should not be understood as 'individualistic' or self-centered. He never loses sight of the social and ecclesial dimension of spiritual doctrine. So in his treatment of the role of the Holy Spirit. The latter not only dwells in each person, but in the entire social body in which personal sanctification is achieved. The first function of the Holy Spirit in the Church is to achieve the unity of its members who are drawn from all nations and all classes of society. Second, the Holy Spirit directs the development of the Church and particularly the development of doctrine. From the beginning He guided the apostles. He inspired the Evangelists 'to record the life of Christ, and directed them which of His words and works to select, which to omit; next, He commented (as it were) upon these, and unfolded their meaning in the Apostolic Epistles. He has made history to be doctrine; telling us plainly, whether by St John or St Paul, that Christ's conception and birth was the real Incarnation of the Eternal Word,—His life, "God manifest in the Flesh,"—His death and resurrection, the Atonement for sin, and the Justification of all believers.' He continued his comment upon it in the formation of the Church and its continuation, and lastly conveys 'this system of Truth, thus varied and expanded to the heart of each individual Christian in whom He dwells.' (PPS II, 19, pp. 226–28)

In the Meditations and Devotions, Newman remarks that it is through the Holy Spirit that 'new religious orders, new devotions in the Church come into being; new countries are added to the faith, new manifestations and illustrations are given of the ancient Apostolic creed.' (MD, p. 397)

Newman often emphasizes that the real life of the Church and of its members is a hidden one. Consequently, with reference to the Evangelicals, he saw in this doctrine of the Divine Indwelling a remedy to stop much of the enthusiasm that prevailed on the part of those who 'place the

life of a Christian, which "is hid with Christ in God," in a sort of religious
ecstasy, in a high-wrought sensibility on sacred subjects . . . and in an
unnatural profession of all this in conversation.' It should also provide, he
said, an answer to those in the Anglican Church known as the High and
Dry, 'sensible and sober-minded men,' who, offended at such excesses,
'acquiesce in the notion, that the gift of the Holy Ghost was almost
peculiar to the Apostles' day, that now, at least, it does nothing more than
make us decent and orderly members of society.' (*PPS* III, 18, p. 268)

Practical Conclusions

Newman drew from the doctrine of the indwelling of the Holy Spirit
some practical spiritual conclusions. First, we must live in the conviction
of God's presence within us. 'In all circumstances, of joy or sorrow, hope
or fear, let us aim at having Him in our inmost heart. . . . Let us submit
ourselves to His guidance and sovereign direction; let us come to Him
that He may forgive us, cleanse us, change us, guide us, and save us. This
is the true life of saints. This is to have the Spirit witnessing with our
spirits that we are sons of God.' (*PPS* V, 16, p. 236)

Second, the thought of the indwelling should make us detached from
worldly objects, such as wealth, luxury, distinctions, popularity, and
power. The Christian ought to be calm and collected under all circumstances, and make light of injuries and forget them. Third, the knowledge of this doctrine excludes all pride. Indeed, it is intimately connected
with the deepest humility, since it is a great gift totally unmerited, and
can be withdrawn because of serious sin. 'Accordingly, the self-respect of
the Christian is no personal and selfish feeling, but rather a principle of
loyal devotion and reverence towards that Divine Master who condescends
to visit him.' It is a powerful motive to avoid sin, for thereby one remains
faithful to the Spirit within, and to sin grievously is to lose His Presence.
This doctrine, when lived, ought to remove gloom and sorrow from the
soul and bathe it in light and joy and peace. The Holy Spirit 'lives in the
Christian's heart, as a never-failing fount of charity. . . . How can charity
towards all men fail to follow? Such a doctrine leads the soul to trust
completely in God's personal Providence over his life and activities, as

well as over the Church despite its sins and imperfections.' (*SD*, 11, pp. 145–48; *PPS* II, 19, p. 230)

Finally, it should fill us with gratitude and love for our Savior who brought all this about through His sacrificial love for us manifested in the total economy of the incarnation.

III The Invisible World

Chapter Seven

The Kingdom of Heaven—
An Invisible World

The Sacramental Presence of Christ

Though Christ ascended into heaven and sits at the right hand of the
Father, He has, in one sense, never left the world since He first entered it,
for, through the agency of the Holy Spirit, He is really present with us
and imparts Himself to those who seek Him, according to His words,
'Behold, I stand at the door and knock. If any man hear My voice, and
open the door, I will come in to him, and will sup with him, and he with
Me.' (Rev. 3:20) In a remarkable passage Newman affirms that 'the hour
of His Cross and Passion [is] ever mystically present, though it is past
these eighteen hundred years. Time and space have no portion in the
spiritual Kingdom which He has founded; and the rites of His Church are
mysterious spells by which He annuls them both.' (*PPS* III, 19, p. 277)

A hundred years before it became usual to speak of the sacraments as
encounters with Christ, Newman propounded the same doctrine.
'Christ,' he affirmed, shines through the sacraments, 'as through transpar-
ent bodies, without impediment.' These mysteries are not mere outward
signs, 'but (as it were) effluences of His grace developing themselves in
external forms, as Angels might do when they appeared to men. . . .
Once for all He hung upon the cross, and blood and water issued from
His pierced side, but by the Spirit's ministration, the blood and water are
ever flowing.' The Christian therefore must look upon the sacraments and
ordinances, not in themselves, 'but as signs of His presence and power, as
the accents of His love, the very form and countenance of Him who ever
beholds us, ever cherishes us.' All of them have life. It is through the

sacraments that Christ communicates His life to us. (*PPS* III, 19, pp. 278–79)

In Baptism the soul puts on Christ, as St Paul says, 'As many of you as have been baptized into Christ, have put on Christ.' (Gal. 1) He also contrasts baptism with the Jewish ceremony of circumcision which it superseded. Baptism is a spiritual circumcision, and therefore invisible, the circumcision of Christ, whereby the soul is buried with Christ. (Col. 2) 'The Baptismal font is called "the washing *of regeneration,*" not of mere water, "and renewing of the Holy Ghost which He hath poured out on us richly through Jesus Christ our Saviour"; and Christ is said to have "loved the Church and given Himself for it, that He might sanctify and cleanse it with the washing of water by the Word, that He might present it to Himself a glorious Church."' Newman also emphasizes that our 'baptism is the seal of our fellowship in the gospel of Christ, of our brotherhood one with another in a divine sonship.' All of this is invisible and hence perceptible only with the eyes of faith. (*PPS* III, 19, pp. 279, 281; MS sermon no. 170)

But the 'greatest and highest of all the Sacramental mysteries,' is that of the Eucharist, for 'Christ, who died and rose again for us, is in it spiritually present, in the fulness of His death and of His resurrection. We call His presence in this Holy Sacrament a spiritual presence, not as if "spiritual" were but a name . . . but by way of expressing that He who is present there can neither be seen nor heard; that He cannot be approached or ascertained by any of the senses; that He is not present in place, that He is not present carnally, though He is really present.' (*PPS* VI, 11, pp. 136–37)

Newman urged his parishioners to the practice of frequent communion and warned them not to use the excuse of unworthiness to omit coming to holy communion, because in doing so 'you lose a mysterious entrance to the Court of the Living God,' a way of approaching Him 'unlike any other way which God has given—higher, more mysterious, more sublime.' Newman then explains in one of the most sublime passages in his sermons:

Suppose yourself to have your eyes wrapt round and to be carried aloft by Angels to the third heaven and laid at the foot of God's throne—Suppose yourself there to lie unable to rise and look about but with the certain knowledge that there you were—that God was there—and Jesus on His right hand—that He was there sitting glorified but in the same body in which He ascended—with the same flesh and blood, though made immortal and spiritual, which He had on earth—with the marks of the nails on it and of the spear—and supposing you were made sensible, though you felt it not, that He drew near to you, and placed His hand upon you, sealing you on the forehead with His Father's name, or placing His cross upon your shoulders or on your breast—And supposing you knew, though still you saw and felt it not, that at His touch virtue went from Him and His Spirit entered into you, and armed you against all the devices of Satan to which your every day life is exposed— Supposing you knew all this and reflected on all this as you lay, though you had no sensible evidence of it, seeing, hearing, feeling nothing, knowing all—Supposing you knew too that all the while your Lord's praises were being sung though you heard them not, by Angels and Archangels, Cherubim and Seraphim who were there—that Apostles and Prophets were there—that Saints were there—close beside you gathered together at the foot of the throne, lay the souls of the multitude of believers whose bodies sleep in the dust of the earth, that there they were lying, close and thick, silent and motionless, though living—what a thought would all this be to you—such a wonderful entrance into the invisible world, though your mortal senses perceived nothing—and then suppose after a while you were suddenly transported back to where you were before, and sent among men again. Would not this be a privilege so great, that great as the awe of it would be, yet desire of it would overcome fear so far as to make you willing to undergo it? (MS sermon no. 459, pp. 7–9, later redaction)

The Eucharistic celebration not only unites us with Christ but with all other Christians as well. 'We are one bread and one body—for we are all partakers of that one bread.' (1 Cor. 10) Hence, it is an expression of love and union with all members of the Church mystically present in Christ. It is a sharing together 'the same bread and the same cup in taking communion together in our Saviour.' (MS sermon no. 172)

It was the common teaching of the Anglican Church, to which New-man subscribed, that though Christ is *really* present in the sacrament, this was not by way of transubstantiation or the changing of the substance of bread into the Body of Christ and that of the wine into His Blood. The bread remained bread, the wine, wine.[1] The belief of Christ present in the blessed sacrament reserved in the tabernacle was one of the great consolations of Newman's life as a Catholic. Writing to Henry Wilberforce in February 1846 he affirmed, 'it is such an incomprehensible blessing to have Christ in bodily presence in one's house . . . as swallows up all other privileges and destroys, or should destroy, every pain.' It sustained him in the greatest pain he experienced in converting, the loss of his friends in the Anglican Church, as it did at other times of intense suffering, for example, at the death of Ambrose St John.[2]

Other Encounters with Christ

But there are other ways than in the sacraments in which Christ is present though invisibly. Public worship and prayer, even if not at a communion service, is such a way, according to the promise of Christ that where two or three are gathered in His name, there He is in the midst of them. So much was this so, that Newman placed a special emphasis upon it. He is also present in His ministers, who despite their faults and failings are representatives of Christ and manifest Him to their flocks. (MS sermon nos. 213 and 191)

Newman emphasized that Christ is present not merely as God but as the Incarnate Word made flesh. As God He is ever present, but how He is present as the Incarnate Word is a great mystery. Newman tried to make this more understandable to his listeners. One way was to remind them that Christ's risen body was spiritualized and to recall the nature of His presence after the resurrection. 'He came and went as He pleased; that material substances, such as the fastened doors, were not impediments to His coming; and that when He was present His disciples did not, as a matter of course, know Him.' (*PPS* VI, sermon 10)

If it is difficult to realize Christ's presence because it is not visible, it is worthwhile to remember, Newman said, that even when on earth Christ was not recognized by those who were closest to him: his relatives who thought Him to be out of His mind, and even His disciples. To Philip He had to say, 'Have I been so long with you, and yet you do not know me, Philip?' And so it is doubtful that if Christ came among us today, many would recognize Him. Perhaps no one so much as Newman emphasized the hiddenness of Christ. At the same time he preached that

Christ is present to us in a more 'real' way than in His earthly life. 'We have lost the sensible and conscious perception of Him; we cannot . . .hear Him, converse with Him, follow Him from place to place; but we enjoy the spiritual, immaterial, inward, mental, real sight and possession of Him; a possession more real and more present than that which the Apostles had in the day of His flesh, *because* it is spiritual, *because* it is invisible.' (*PPS* IV, sermons 16 and 17; VI, 10, p. 121)

Such encounters with Christ in the invisible world, which are encounters in faith, should stir up in us feelings of both joy and fear, fear in the biblical sense of reverence, for the majesty of Christ. Such feelings we will have only if we *realize* His presence. 'In proportion as we believe that He is present, we shall have them; and not to have them, is not to realize, not to believe that He is present.' If one feels His presence, then one 'will shrink from addressing Him familiarly, or using before Him unreal words . . . or addressing Him in a familiar posture of body.' One will prepare in advance for the reception of the Eucharist. St Paul, after discoursing on faith as 'the realizing of things hoped for, the evidence of things not seen,' adds: 'let us have grace, whereby we may serve God acceptably with reverence and godly fear.' (*PPS* V, 2, pp. 22–27) (For the meaning of 'unreal words,' see *PPS* V, 3, pp. 29–43)

Moreover, these encounters with Christ are necessary as a preparation for meeting Him later when we stand before Him in judgment. Consequently, one should look upon religious services as 'going out to meet the Bridegroom.' One should come to Church therefore to learn 'to endure the sight of the Holy One and His servants; to nerve myself for a vision which is fearful before it is ecstatic, and which they only enjoy whom it does not consume.' The ceremonies we see force the unseen truth upon our senses, so even those who live more to the world than to God feel the effect of coming to the weekly services, for it is a 'continual memento on their conscience, giving them a glimpse of things unseen.' In time they grow to be different persons. 'The very disposition of the building, the subdued light, the aisles, the Altar, with its pious adornments, are figures of things unseen, and stimulate our fainting faith.' (*PPS* V, 1, pp. 7–9; III, 17, pp. 251–52)

It should be recalled too that though a thick veil is spread between this world and the invisible world, still at times there are 'marvellous disclosures made to us of what is behind it.' Newman describes one such disclosure which seems like, and may very well have been, a mystical experience. He writes:

> At times we seem to catch a glimpse of a Form which we shall hereafter see face to face. We approach, and in spite of the darkness, our hands, or our head, or our brow, or our lips become, as it were, sensible of the contact of something more than earthly. We know not where we are, but we have been bathing in water, and a voice tells us that it is blood. Or we have a mark signed upon our foreheads, and it spoke of Calvary. Or we recollect a hand laid upon our heads, and surely it had the print of nails in it, and resembled His who with a touch gave sight to the blind and raised the dead. Or we have been eating and drinking; and it was not a dream surely, that One fed us from His wounded side, and renewed our nature by the heavenly meat He gave. Thus in many ways He, who is Judge to us, prepares us to be judged,—He, who is to glorify us, prepares us to be glorified, that He may not take us unawares; but that when the voice of the Archangel sounds, and we are called to meet the Bridegroom, we may be ready. (*PPS* V, 1, pp. 10–11)

The Communion of Saints

Not only Christ inhabits the invisible world of heaven, but God, the angels, the apostles, and all the elect who have died, the saints. The visible Church on earth is really part of a larger unit. The true ecclesial community is 'that great invisible company, who are one and all incorporated in the one mystical body of Christ, and quickened by one Spirit.' (*PPS* IV, 11, p. 174) The visible and invisible Church are fundamentally one, the convex and concave of the same reality. 'We do not make two Churches, we only view the Christian body as existing in the world of Spirits; and the present Church visible, so far as it really has part and lot in the same blessedness.' (*PPS* III, 16, pp. 222–23) In this visible Church, which has existed from the time it was set up at Pentecost, the invisible Church is gradually molded and matured. (*PPS* III, 17, pp. 240–41)

Newman stresses that the redemptive work of Christ can be applied to the individual only in a social and ecclesial way. 'The whole Church living and dead is bound together in one communion and whenever we baptize our children, or receive the Blessed Eucharist we admit souls and advance deeper into the fellowship of the dead as well as the living.' (MS sermon no. 389) This visible community of the Church on earth should be 'as a guide to what is inward, something visible as a guide to what is spiritual . . . which directs and leads us to the very Holy of Holies, in which Christ dwells by His Spirit.' (*PPS* IV, 11, pp. 173–75)

Since there exists this bond of union between all Christians since the time of the apostles, a bond of union, created by the action of the Holy Spirit, there is an objective communion between the living and the dead. Consequently, 'we are not solitary, though we seem so. . . . Those multitudes in the primitive time, who believed, and taught and worshipped, as we do, still live unto God. . . . They animate us by their example; they cheer us by their company; they are on our right hand and our left, Martyrs, Confessors, and the like, high and low, who used the same Creeds, and celebrated the same Mysteries, and preached the same Gospel as we do.' (*PPS* III, 25, pp. 385–86) They are at rest, but 'active promoters of the Church's welfare, as by prayer.' Nevertheless, Newman's Anglican principles would not allow him to go so far as to recommend the living to invoke the aid of the saints. First, because the practice, he said, was not primitive. Second, because we are told to pray to God alone, 'invocation may easily be corrupted into prayer, and then become idolatrous.' We are therefore to think of them, yet not to speak to them. (*PPS* IV, 11, pp. 182–83) This is a good example of the appositiveness of Maisie Ward's observation that the Tractarians were hedged with cautions lest they slip at any time from the *via media*.[3]

As a Catholic Newman felt no such restraint. Writing to a recent convert to the Catholic Church, he said, 'I recollect how I rejoiced myself on my reception into the Church at being at length under the feet of the Saints and able without introduction or ceremony to address them and make sure of their sympathy.' (N to Mrs Lee, 2 April 1881, *LD* XXIX, p. 357) The joy at being able to invoke Our Lady and the saints is evident in various letters he wrote after becoming a Catholic. In one letter to an enquirer who was disturbed by 'Mariolatry' and 'Saint Worship,' Newman composed an explanation of a Catholic's faith:

> We believe in a family of God, of which the Saints are the heavenly members and we the earthly—yet one family embracing earth and heav-

en. We believe we have access to the heavenly members, and are at liberty to converse with them—and that we can ask them for benefits and they can gain them for us. We believe at the same time that they are so different from us, and so much above us, that our natural feelings towards them would be awe, fear, and dismay, such as we should have on seeing a ghost, or as Daniel's when he fell down and quaked at the vision of the Angel—these feelings being changed into loving admiration and familiar devotion, by our belief in the Communion of Saints. Moreover, we believe them present with us as truly as our fellow-men are present. Now consider the honours paid to monarchs on earth—men kneel to them, bow to their empty throne, pay them the most profound homage, use almost the language of slaves in addressing them, and dare not approach them without a ceremonial. Much more reverently ought the Saints to be treated by us, in proportion as heaven is higher than earth— yet I do not think we observe that proportion—our language towards our Lady and the Saints is not so much above that which is used towards great personages on earth, as immortal blessedness is above temporal power. (N to E. Berdoe, 2 October 1865, *LD* XXII, pp. 64–65)

What the visible temple was to the Jews, that and much more is the invisible kingdom of heaven to us. It is a refuge from the world, a hiding-place, a home for the lonely. 'Let us disappear in the spiritual kingdom of our God. . . . What fellowship can be more glorious, more satisfying than that which we may hold with those inmates of the City of God. . . . Leave then this earthly scene . . . aim at a higher prize, a nobler companionship. Enter into the Tabernacle of God. . . . Though thou art in a body of flesh, a member of this world, thou hast but to kneel down reverently in prayer, and thou art at once in the society of Saints and Angels.' (*PPS* IV, 12, pp. 191–98)

This kingdom of God is among us. 'We look,' says St Paul, 'not at the things which are seen; but at the things which are not seen; for the things which are seen are temporal, but the things which are not seen are eternal.' Eternity is not distant, because it reaches to the future; nor is the unseen state without influence on us, because it is impalpable. So St Paul also says, 'our conversation is in heaven,' and 'your life is hid with Christ in God,' and St Peter, 'Whom having seen, ye love; in whom though now ye see Him not, yet believing, ye rejoice with joy unspeakable and full of glory.'

The Coming of the Kingdom

This is the hidden kingdom of God which will one day appear suddenly as the angels appeared to the shepherds. 'Bright as is the sun, and the sky, and the clouds; sweet as is the singing of the birds; they are not all. . . . They proceed from a centre of love and goodness, which is God himself. . . . they speak of heaven but are not heaven; they are stray beams and dim reflections of His Image. . . . We know that what we see is as a screen hiding from us God and Christ, and His Saints and Angels. And we earnestly desire and pray for the dissolution of all that we see, from our longing after that which we do not see.' (*PPS* IV, 12, pp. 208–11)

This invisible world, which will be completed when the visible world comes to an end, is perceived only through the eyes of faith. 'What we see is the outward shell of an eternal kingdom; and on that Kingdom we fix the eyes of faith.' And by faith Newman means what Scott called 'living faith,' that is, in Newman's terminology, 'real apprehension,' and moreover a faith that has become habitual. Thus, he writes in one long but beautiful passage how the things we see should speak to us of those things which are to come when the beauty of the visible world recedes before the beauty of the invisible:

> To those who live by faith, every thing they see speaks of that future world; the very glories of nature, the sun, moon, and stars, and the richness and the beauty of the earth, are as types and figures witnessing and teaching the invisible things of God. All that we see is destined one day to burst forth into a heavenly bloom, and to be transfigured into immortal glory. Heaven at present is out of sight, but in due time, as snow melts and discovers what it lay upon, so will this visible creation fade away before those greater splendours which are behind it, and on which at present it depends. In that day shadows will retire, and the substance show itself. The sun will grow pale and be lost in the sky, but it will be before the radiance of Him whom it does but image, the Sun of Righteousness, with healing on His wings, who will come forth in visible form, as a bridegroom out of his chamber, while His perishable type decays. The stars which surround it will be replaced by Saints and Angels circling His throne. Above and below, the clouds of the air, the trees of the field, the waters of the great deep will be found impregnated with the forms of everlasting spirits, the servants of God which do His

pleasure. And our own mortal bodies will then be found in like manner to contain within them an inner man, which will then receive its due proportions, as the soul's harmonious organ, instead of that gross mass of flesh and blood which sight and touch are sensible of. For this glorious manifestation the whole creation is at present in travail, earnestly desiring that it may be accomplished in its season. (*PPS* IV, 14, pp. 223–24)

Such thoughts, Newman asserts, urge the Christian to look forward to this future coming, to try and hasten it, rejoicing that every day and hour that passes bring us closer to the time of His appearing, 'and the termination of sin and misery.' (*PPS* IV, 14, pp. 223–24) He describes the joy with which we will awaken to the vision of eternal life, 'gifted with fresh powers . . . able to love God as we wish, conscious that all trouble, sorrow, pain, anxiety, bereavement is over for ever, blessed in the full affection of those earthly friends whom we loved so poorly, and could protect so feebly, while they were with us in the flesh, and above all, visited by the immediate visible ineffable Presence of God Almighty, with his Only-begotten Son our Lord Jesus Christ, and His Co-equal Co-eternal Spirit, that great sight in which is the fulness of joy and pleasure for evermore,—what deep, incommunicable, unimaginable thoughts will be then upon us! . . . Earthly words are indeed all worthless to minister to such high anticipations. Let us close our eyes and keep silence.' (*PPS* IV, 14, pp. 212–13)

Notes

1. No attempt has been made in this chapter to cover the history and development of Newman's views on Baptism and the Eucharist. Studies of these have been done by Thomas Sheridan, S. J., *Newman on Justification*, Staten Island 1967; and A. Hardelin, *The Tractarian Understanding of the Eucharist*, Uppsala 1965. See also *VM* II, 145–257.

2. To H. W. Wilberforce, 26 February 1846, *LD* XI, p. 129. To Isaac Williams, 21 October 1861, to W. J. Copeland, 23 January 1863, to Charles Robbins, 20 May 1863, *LD* XX, pp. 59–60, 400, 449. Cf. 'Loyalty of Cardinal Newman,' The *Month* 70 (November 1890), 306–7.

3. Maisie Ward, *Young Mr Newman*, London 1952, p. 339.

Chapter Eight

The Role of Mary

GOD COULD have redeemed man from his fallen state and reconciled him to Himself without becoming man, but once the incarnation was decreed, its economy included, as has been seen, the atonement on the cross, His resurrection from the dead, His ascension into heaven, and His communication of the fruits of the redemption through the Holy Spirit by means of the sacraments and the Church. By the incarnation the Word was made flesh; He was conceived and born of a woman, and she was destined to be associated with Him, not just by giving birth to Him, but in the total economy of the incarnation.

Just as Christ's redemptive action was a free fulfillment of His Father's will, so Mary's conception of the Word was an act of complete obedience and surrender to the divine will. 'It was God's will that she should undertake *willingly* and with *full understanding* to be the Mother of our Lord, and not to be a mere passive instrument whose maternity would have no merit and no reward. . . . It was no light lot to be so intimately near to the Redeemer of men, as she experienced afterwards when she suffered with him. Therefore, weighing well the Angel's words before giving her answer to them—first she asked whether so great an office would be a forfeiture of that Virginity which she had vowed. When the Angel told her no, then, with the full consent of a full heart, full of God's love to her and her own lowliness, she said, "Behold the handmaid of the Lord; be it done unto me according to thy word."'

This perfect obedience to God's will was emphasized by the Fathers of the Church in calling her the Second Eve, 'as having taken the first step in the salvation of mankind which Eve took in its ruin.' St Irenaeus, for example, affirmed, 'As Eve, becoming disobedient, became *the cause* of death to herself and *to all mankind, so* Mary, too, bearing the predestined Man, and yet a Virgin, being obedient, became the CAUSE OF SALVATION both to herself and to all mankind.' The same author concluded his comparison with a statement about the obedience and faith of Mary: 'the knot formed by Eve's disobedience was untied by the obedience of Mary; that what the Virgin Eve tied through unbelief, that the Virgin Mary unties through faith.' (*MD*, pp. 82–83. See also *Diff.* II, 34–35)

In the treating of Our Lady and her privileges Newman invoked, in addition to the Fathers of the Church, the principle that Christian doctrine forms one whole and that the parts are harmoniously combined. They fit together. Thus, even historically the incarnation of the Second Person of the Trinity and Mary as the Mother of God were intimately conjoined. When the denial of the divinity of Christ was implied by the Arians, 'the Church, guided by God, would find no more effectual and sure way of expelling them, than that of the using the word *Deipara*, or Mother of God, against them.' (*Mix.*, pp. 333–34, 360–61) Thus from this one doctrine of Mary, the Mother of God, Newman showed how all her privileges flow: her sanctity, her Immaculate Conception, her dignity, her power of intercession, and her stature as an object of devotion. One other doctrine Newman showed to be appropriate and harmonized with the rest was Mary's Assumption into heaven, for without it 'Catholic teaching would have a character of incompleteness.' (*Mix.*, p. 361)

Mary's Holiness and Her Immaculate Conception

Mary's sanctity, Newman affirmed, comes, not only of her being Mother of the Incarnate Word, 'but also His being her son.' No limits 'but those proper to a creature can be assigned to the sanctity of Mary.' It must surpass that of all the saints. The very fact that certain privileges are known to have been theirs persuades us, almost from the necessity of the case, that she had the same and higher. 'Her conception was immaculate in order that she might surpass all Saints in the date as well as the fulness of her sanctification.' (*Mix.*, pp. 369–70)

Adam and Eve were originally endowed with grace beyond nature. 'If then Eve was raised above human nature by the indwelling of what we call grace, is it rash to say that Mary had even greater grace?' This is the meaning of the greeting of the angel to Mary, 'full of grace,' if one holds with the doctrine of the Fathers that it is an inward condition or quality of the soul, and 'not a mere external approbation or acceptance.' And if Eve had this supernatural inward gift from the first moment of her existence, is it possible to deny that Mary too had this gift from the very moment of her personal existence? This, however, argues Newman, is to imply the doctrine of the Immaculate Conception. (*Diff.* II, 45–46)

To the objection how does this enable us to say Mary was conceived without original sin, Newman replies that original sin is not actual sin, but the condition of Adam and Eve when they lost original grace. It is a condition of soul, something negative, not positive. It is the absence of supernatural life, and this state is transmitted to Adam and Eve's descendants. Mary could not merit, any more than they, the restoration of that grace; but it was restored by God's free bounty, from the first moment of her existence. Hence, she never came under the original curse, which consisted in the loss of it.

Mary had this special privilege to prepare her to become the mother of *her* and *our* Redeemer, 'to fit her mentally and spiritually for it. As a consequence by the aid of this first grace, she was enabled to grow in grace, that, when the angel came and our Lord was at hand, she might be "full of grace," prepared as far as a creature could be prepared, to receive Him.' Consequently, although Mary could *not* merit the first grace of *Immaculate Conception,* she could merit by her faith and her obedience the gift of being the *Mother* of our Redeemer.

What the Immaculate Conception does *not* mean is that the Blessed Virgin did not die in Adam, that she did not come under the penalty of the fall, that she was not redeemed. Had this been clearly understood, earlier opposition to the definition of the doctrine would not have occurred. As Newman remarked elsewhere, 'When all seemed lost, in order . . . to reverse all the consequences of the Fall, our Lord began, even before His coming, to do His most wonderful act of redemption, in the person of her who was to be His Mother. By the merit of that Blood which was to be shed, He interposed to hinder her incurring the sin of Adam, before He had made on the Cross atonement for it.' (*Diff.* II, 47–50; *MD,* p. 11)

Mary's Growth

All through her life Mary grew in faith and love of Christ and in holiness. Commenting on the text, 'But Mary kept all these things, and pondered them in her heart,' Newman sees Mary as *the* pattern of faith and of its development in the Church, because developments result from the realization of the truths of faith:

> St Mary is our pattern of Faith, both in the reception and in the study of Divine Truth. She does not think it enough to accept, she dwells upon it . . . not enough to assent, she develops it; not enough to submit the Reason, she reasons upon it; not indeed reasoning first, and believing afterwards, with Zacharias, yet first believing without reasoning, next from love and reverence, reasoning after believing. And thus she symbolizes to us, not only the faith of the unlearned, but of the doctors of the Church also. (*OUS*, p. 313)

Never did Mary sin even venially, in thought, word, or deed. She remained 'the most Faithful Virgin,' being true to Him unto the end. Great as was the devotion to our Lord of the saints such as St Paul, who said, 'I know nothing but Jesus Christ and Him crucified,' much greater was that of the Blessed Virgin 'because she was His Mother, and because she had Him and all His sufferings actually before her eyes, and because she had the long intimacy of thirty years with Him, and because she was from her personal sanctity ineffably near to Him in Spirit.' (*MD*, p. 51)

At His passion she was present and suffered with Him; her suffering, however, was 'not in the body but in the soul. . . . She suffered a fellow-passion; she was crucified with Him; the spear that pierced His breast pierced through her spirit.' (*MD*, p. 53) When the apostles deserted Him, 'it is expressly noted of her that she *stood* by the cross. She *stood upright* to receive the blows, the stabs, which the long Passion of her Son inflicted upon her every moment.' What St Paul said of Christ that having suffered and been tempted He was able to succor those who also are tempted, so Mary by reason of her suffering has been called 'the Comforter of the Afflicted.' (*MD*, p. 61)

Glorification of Mary

Having shared in her Son's sufferings it was fitting that she should share in His triumph. So by her Assumption she was taken up to heaven upon her death, both body and soul, so that there was no long period in the grave waiting for the final resurrection of the bodies of the saints. 'Christ's love of His mother of itself would explain it, but also she was so transcendently holy, so full, so overflowing with grace.' Again Newman compares her to Eve: 'If Eve, the beautiful daughter of God, never would have become dust and ashes unless she had sinned, shall we not say that Mary, having never sinned, retained the gift which Eve by sinning lost?' In heaven she is crowned Queen of angels and saints, and joins her Son, who sitting at the right hand of His Father intercedes for those He has redeemed. (*MD*, p. 65ff.)

In her heavenly existence Newman sees the same contrast between Eve, on the one hand, and the woman and the child in the 12th chapter of the Apocalypse, on the other: 'A great sign appeared in heaven: a woman clothed with the Sun, and the Moon under her feet; and on her head a crown of twelve stars. And being with child, she cried travailing in birth, and was in pain to be delivered. And there was seen another sign in heaven and behold a great red dragon.' Thus, not only Mother and Child, but a serpent is introduced into the vision. 'Such a meeting of man, woman, and serpent has not been found in Scripture, since the beginning of Scripture, and now is found in the end.'

Without denying that under the image of the woman the Church is signified, and that this is the direct or real sense of the image, Newman maintained that the Scriptures are not given to personifications, but refer to persons. Hence, he says, 'St John would not have spoken of the Church, *unless* there had existed a blessed Virgin Mary, who was exalted on high, and the object of veneration to all the faithful.' That she was so venerated Newman concludes from the extant pictures of Mother and Child in the Roman catacombs, the earliest of which Cavaliere de Rossi, one of the authorities on the catacombs, believed to be referable to the very age of the apostles.[1] 'Mary is there drawn with the Divine Infant in her lap, she with hand extended in prayer, He with His hand in the attitude of blessing.' (*Diff.* II, 53–61)

From the earliest days of the Church intercessory prayer was prac-ticed. When St Peter was in prison and his life in danger, 'prayer was made without ceasing by the Church of God for him.' In a sermon on intercession, Newman affirmed that it is especially the prerogative and privilege of the obedient and the holy. This truth is brought out in Scripture, for example, in the words of the blind man, 'if any man be a worshipper of God, him He hears.' And the Apostle Paul, 'the prayer of a just man avails much,' and 'whatever we ask, we receive, because we keep his commandments.' So as the ideas of Mary's sanctity and dignity pene-trated the mind of Christendom, so did that of her intercessory power follow close upon it. Far from eclipsing her son's divinity, she brings out his divinity. 'Our Lord cannot pray for us, as a mere creature can, as Mary prays. To her belongs, as being a creature, a natural claim on our sympa-thy and familiarity, in that she is nothing else than our fellow. . . . We look to her without fear, any remorse, any consciousness that she is able to read us, judge us, punish us.' (*Diff.* II, 68–73)

Devotion to Our Lady

As an Anglican Newman was devoted to Our Lady, but in accordance with Anglican principles, he approved Mary's intercession but not direct invocation of her, because he considered that in practice this led in the Roman Church to so-called Mariolatry, or giving to Mary the worship due only to God. After studying Catholic devotional writings about Our Lady, given him by Dr Russell of Maynooth, he was astonished to see how little there was in them that he could object to. After he became a Catholic, he was aware that Marian devotions might create a problem for prospective converts. Writing to Mrs William Froude he enunciated the distinction between Catholic faith regarding Our Lady, which is common to all, on the one hand, and on the other, devotions to her which varied from country to country, individual to individual, and at different times in the history of the Church. The same distinction he made in answer to Pusey's objections to Marian devotion in the Catholic Church. In his *Letter to Pusey* he wrote that by doctrine, belief, or faith, he meant both the content of belief, for example, as set down in the Creed, and also the assent to that content. He defined devotion as 'such honours as belong to the objects of our faith, and the payment of those honours.' They are distinct both in fact and idea. In the Catholic Church 'the faith is everywhere one and the same, but a large liberty is accorded to private judgment and inclination as regards matters of devotion.' (*LD* XVI, 341–42; *Diff.* II, 26–31)

In answer to Pusey Newman remarked, 'There is a healthy devotion to the Blessed Mary, and there is an artificial; it is possible to love her as a Mother, to honour her as a Virgin, to seek her as a Patron, and to exalt her as a Queen, without any injury to solid piety and Christian good sense:— I cannot help calling this the English style.' He then repudiated the exaggerated statements cited by Pusey, 'when taken in their literal and absolute sense,' such sentences as 'that the mercy of Mary is infinite; that God has resigned in her hands His omnipotence; that it is safer to seek her than to seek her Son; that the Blessed Virgin is superior to God.' These sentiments Newman confesses he never knew until he read them in Pusey's work, 'nor, as I think, do the vast majority of English Catholics know them.' (*Diff.* II, 100, 113–14)

The seventy pages of meditations on the Litany of Loretto for the month of May, which Newman composed, are models of theological accuracy and of heartfelt personal love and devotion. Long before Pope Leo XIII instituted the regular preaching of the rosary and October as a month of devotion to her, Newman had introduced daily recitation of the rosary in his own church of the Oratory in Birmingham. In the meditation on Mary Help of Christians for 29 May Newman enumerated five services of Mary's intercession for the 'elect people of God upon earth, and to His holy Church,' four of which were explicitly connected with the rosary: St Dominic's arresting the Albigensian heresy in southern France after he instituted the practice of saying the rosary; the victory of the Christian fleet over 'the powerful Turkish Sultan'; the victory won at Vienna over 'the most savage Sultan of the Turks'; and the victory over the same Turks in Hungary.

It was, however, not so much saying the rosary as a form of petition for Mary's intercession that appealed to Newman; rather it was the opportunity it presented of meditating on the full range of the Christian mysteries, with which Mary was so intimately connected—the economy of the incarnation in its entire scope. This is another example of Newman's recognition that Mary is not the rival of her Son, but 'the handmaid of the Lord,' His servant, and as such her glories were for the sake of her Son. As an Anglican he had used this to explain Mary's hiddenness. In a sermon in 1832 he remarked that little is said about her in the Gospels, and when she departed from this earth, 'we hear no more of her.' Having come to recognize the development of doctrine about Our Lady in the history of the Church, he nuanced this view in his Catholic sermon, 'The Glories of Mary for the sake of Her Son,' when he asserted that 'as she had increased day by day in grace and merit at Nazareth, while the world knew her not, so has she . . . grown into her place in the Church by a tranquil influence and a natural process . . . as some fair tree, stretching forth her fruitful branches and her fragrant leaves, and overshadowing the territory of the Saints.' (PPS II, 12, p. 134; Mix., pp. 357–58)

Pattern of Holiness

Mary plays an important role in Newman's spirituality, not only as an object of veneration and as an advocate who can intercede with her Son, but also as providing after Christ the most perfect model of perfection and of sanctity. She is the 'mirror of justice,' that is, the mirror of sanctity. Her virtues are reflections of His, and so Newman exhorted his listeners:

> Let us copy her faith, who received God's message by the Angel without a doubt; her patience, who endured St Joseph's surprise without a word; her obedience, who went up to Bethlehem in the winter and bore our Lord in a stable; her meditative spirit, who pondered in her heart what she saw and heard about Him; . . .her self-surrender, who gave Him up during His ministry and consented to His death. (Mix, pp. 374–75)

Newman concluded the sermon from which the above extract is taken by saying, 'She is the personal type and representative image of that spiritual life and renovation in grace, "without which no-one shall see God."'

Note

1. Dates for individual works of art in the catacombs vary with different scholars. Some scholars date the portrait of the Madonna and the Child with the prophet Balaam in the cemetery of Priscilla as early as the second century. See Herbert A. Musurillo, ed., *The Fathers of the Primitive Church,* New York 1966, p. 112.

Chapter Nine

The Angels: Service and Praise

Mary reigns in heaven with her Son, but they are surrounded by angels who praise and administer to them.

ONE CANNOT READ very far in Newman's sermons without encountering mention of the angels, often by way of comparison. This is not surprising. From his childhood imaginings about the angels until his old age when he preached so vividly about them that some parishioners left the church convinced he had seen them, Newman maintained a keen sense of and close contact with these inhabitants of the invisible world. No saint has ever nor can ever achieve the natural and supernatural perfection of these extraordinary beings, and Newman found it hard to understand why they were often neglected.

That the angels form a part of the unseen world, he said, appears from the vision seen by the patriarch Jacob, who when he fled from his brother Esau, lay down to sleep. 'He dreamed, and behold, a ladder set up on the earth, and the top of it reached up to heaven; and behold, the Angels of God ascending and descending on it. And behold, the Lord stood above it.' Jacob was shown that this world existed around him, even though he had not known it: 'Angels were all about him, though he knew it not. And what Jacob saw in his sleep, that Elisha's servant saw as if with his eyes; and the shepherds, at the time of the Nativity, not only saw but heard. They heard the voices of those blessed spirits who praise God day and night, and whom we, in our lower state of being, are allowed to copy and assist.' (*PPS* IV, 13, pp. 204–5)

Newman poses the question, why are we told about the angels in Scripture? Surely, he replied, 'for practical purposes.' What purposes? 'In addition to heaven as the palace of the Almighty and of His Son as Saviour the angels are revealed to us, that heaven may be as little as possible an unknown place in our imaginations.' Nevertheless, Newman cautions, 'contemplation of the angels should not be a mere feeling, and a sort of luxury of the imagination.' The thought of thousands upon thousands of ministering spirits standing before God, so infinitely higher in the scale of being than we, should impress the mind with a realization of the majesty of God, 'how high then must be the Lord of Angels! The very Seraphim hide their faces before His glory, while they praise Him.' (*PPS* II, 29, pp. 365–67)

These remarks are taken from the sermon, 'The Powers of Nature,' first preached on 29 September 1831, the Feast of St Michael. In part it was based upon the doctrine of the Alexandrian Fathers of the Church, whom he was studying at the time. From them, as he acknowledged in the *Apologia* (*Apo.*, p. 28), he learned to think of the angels 'as the real causes of motion, light, and life.' He affirms that the investigations of science need not be supposed to have superseded this view, and hence nature should be approached with reverence. He asks, what would be the thoughts of a man, who, 'when examining a flower, or a herb, or a pebble, or a ray of light . . . suddenly discovered he was in the presence of some powerful being who was hidden behind the visible things he was inspecting, who, though concealing his wise hand, was giving them their beauty, grace, and perfections, as being God's instrument for the purpose?' He urges his hearers, therefore, to make the visible world a means of reminding them of these beings in the invisible world. 'Thus, whenever we look abroad, we are reminded of those gracious and holy Beings, the servants of the Holiest, who deign to minister to the heirs of salvation. Every breath of air and ray of light and heat, every beautiful prospect is, as it were, the skirts of their garments.' (*PPS* II, 29, pp. 362–64)

Newman found it hard to understand on the one hand disbelief and skepticism about the angels, and on the other, fear of idolatry on the part of adherents to Bible religion, especially when Scripture is filled with references to them. In fact, 'there is much more about the Blessed Angels in Scripture than about many of those doctrines which we think, and rightly think, most important. We hear of them from the beginning of the Bible to the end—and in the first book and in the last. . . . It so happens that Angels accompany all the providences, all the dispensations of God, so that nothing is told us about Him but something is added of them also. Are we told that God is the Creator of all things? we are told

that at the creation "all the sons of God" or Angels "shouted for joy."—
Are we told that Christ shall judge us? He will come with His "holy
Angels." '

St Michael and the Angels: Their Care of Holy Men

In MS sermon no. 260, 'St Michael and the angels—their guardianship
and care of the saints,' preached on 29 September 1830 and repeated on
the same day in 1832, 1837, and 1841, Newman traces references to the
angels throughout the whole of Scripture. What do we learn from all
this? That the angels were put to a test and that some stood and some fell,
that the latter were cast into hell. For what reason, Newman asks, was the
existence of the bad angels revealed? He answers, 'to excite our fear, to
increase our vigilance, and to rouse us to fight for our prize with zeal,'
while we are told of the existence of *good* angels 'for our comfort and
instruction.' From the beginning, when they were stationed at the gate of
Paradise to prevent fallen man from returning, they were thereafter employed in similar offices of judgment and punishment, for example, in the
fiery overthrow of Sodom and Gomorrah, the death of the firstborn in
Egypt, the pestilence on David's numbering the people, and the destruction of Sennacherib's army, 'deeds sudden, resistless, overwhelming,'—
'the memorials of their strength.' By comparison, what are human power
and human skill? In fear of but one of them the keepers of the holy
sepulchre shook and became as dead men. These were pagan soldiers, but
even the servants of God such as Daniel were struck with terror before the
holy angels.

Revelations about the angels were not restricted to incidents which
displayed their strength; they have been implicated in the management of
the world's affairs. Like the Lord of angels Himself, 'they condescend to
minister to men, in one sense to be *servants* of good men, to supply their
wants, to guard them and warn them—to aid them individually.' From
time to time in the Old Testament the outer veil that shields the angels
from our sight was removed, so that angels were seen to walk the earth, to
discourse with men and to lodge with them. Hence the reason that St
Paul gives for exercising hospitality: 'Be not forgetful to entertain strangers, for thereby some have entertained angels unawares!' (Heb. 13)

From the time of Abraham to that of Samuel (later succeeded by the prophets) they often appear to good men in human form, for example, the three angels who appeared to Abraham and were addressed as travelers and he supplied them with food and drink. Sometimes they revealed themselves before they disappeared, for example, to Gideon. So also in the mysterious account of Jacob's wrestling with one who turns out to be an angel. Though they are only sometimes made visible, they are always there, for when God opened the eyes of the young servant of Elisha, he saw that the mountain was filled with chariots of fire and horses of fire around Elisha. (2 Kings 6)[1]

Though hidden from our eyes, the angels nevertheless minister to us constantly. In fact, as Christians we have more direct promises of their assistance than the Jews had. First, there is our Lord's assurance 'there is joy in the presence of the angels of God over one sinner that repenteth.' (Luke 15) They are sent purposely to help and protect the children of God, as St Paul remarks, 'Are they not all ministering spirits sent forth to minister for them who shall be heirs of salvation.' (Heb. 1:14) Our Lord bids us not to despise one of His little ones, His weak and young disciples, 'for I say unto you that in heaven *their angels* do always behold the face of My Father,' that is, their guardian angels. (Matt. 18) Lazarus is carried by angels into Abraham's bosom—again St Paul urges reverence in God's house because of the presence of angels.

There is no contradiction in saying that the angels are both in heaven and on earth, for what is heaven but God's presence, and He is everywhere. Doubtless heaven is also a place where the Son of God resides at the right hand of the Father, but the angels being spirits can come and go from heaven to earth. In accordance with the recommendation of St Paul, who charged Timothy to act 'before God and the Lord Jesus Christ and the elect angels,' we should live in their presence, conscious that they are witnessing all we do, beings created like us but who have stood the test of temptation and are perfected in holiness. We are even now surrounded by those who are destined to be our future associates in heaven, who in turn are looking with interest at us all, 'to see *how many* of man's corrupt race God will bring to glory, and who do their part to lead us thither.'

The thought of the presence of the angels can help us avoid sin, for it is 'a check for all forms of indulgence, all deviations from strictest temperance and purity, to think that we may be yoked with an immortal angel who neither comprehends the excesses of human passions, nor can endure their defilement.' All this was summed up in a poem to his Guardian Angel which Newman published for the first time in *Verses on Religious Subjects*, 1853. The final verses are developed at some length in the dialogue between the departed soul and his guardian angel in the *Dream of Gerontius*. (VRS, pp. 12–14; VV, pp. 334–70)

Strength and Protection of the Angels (MS sermon no. 540)

Since the angels are invisible, Newman not only had to convince his hearers of their existence and activities but to make them realize this. As so often he had recourse to analogy. Preaching on the feast of St Michael, 29 September 1838, on a text from Daniel 10, in which Daniel is given a vision of an angel, Newman in a somewhat wordy and repetitious introduction, develops a detailed account of the interdependence of all members of society and all different occupations so as to achieve society's welfare. Some of these occupations are specifically ordered to the protection of citizens, such as 'civil officers, magistrates, and judges', who are 'the protectors of society, repressing crime, and saving us from robbery, murder, and other evils.' Not just children but grown-ups are under the guidance, governance, and safe-keeping of others. He then poses the question, Has God appointed any of His creatures to protect and support these persons as they protect and support their brethren? He answers in the affirmative, 'He has appointed, though we see them not, He has appointed, as the Bible shows, His holy Angels.'

Some of the angels are more powerful than the greatest of kings and warriors—far more holy than the holiest of God's friends and therefore fit protectors of the powerful and the holy. The text from Daniel 10:5, 6 describes how powerful and holy they are, 'or in a word how glorious.' 'I lifted up mine eyes and looked and behold a certain man clothed in linen, whose loins were girded with fine gold of Uphaz; his body also was like the beryl, and his face as the appearance of lightning, and his eyes as lamps of fire, and his arms and his feet like in colour to polished brass,— and the voice of his words like the voice of a multitude.'

Newman exegeted the text as follows: 'His golden girdle is meant to show his great perfection, his excellence in God's sight—and how highly

God prized him. His body was like a precious stone called the beryl—and his face like lightning, and his eyes like fire, and his arms and his feet like brass; all this marks his exceedingly great purity, sanctity and heavenliness.—And his voice was like the voice of a multitude—This intimates his great power.' The angel's power and strength are evident from the effect of his presence on the men who were with the prophet, though they saw him not. 'A great quaking fell upon them, so that they fled to hide themselves.' A similar effect was later produced on the soldiers who guarded Christ's tomb. 'His countenance was like lightning and his raiment white as snow. And for fear of him the keepers did shake and become as dead men.' (Matt. 28) How holy the angel was, Newman affirms, is plain from the effect of the vision on Daniel himself, who was an especially holy man. 'There remained no strength in me,' he said.

Daniel is instructed, strengthened, and comforted by angels. In the previous chapter, the angel tells him, 'O Daniel, a man greatly beloved, understand the words I speak unto thee, and stand upright—for unto thee am I now sent.' And then Daniel comments, 'He strengthened me and said, O man greatly beloved, fear not: peace be unto thee; be strong, yea be strong.' In like manner in another place it is said that after he had been fasting, praying, and confessing the angel Gabriel came and said, 'O Daniel, I am come forth to give thee skill and understanding.'

This powerful angel also protects the powerful. For example, in the first verse of the next chapter it is said, 'also I in the first year of Darius the Mede (who was king) even I stood to confirm and to strengthen him.' And again in the fourth chapter King Nebuchadnezzar is watched over by two angels whom he saw in a dream, and who are called 'a watcher and a holy one.'

Not only do the angels watch over great men and holy men, they watch over all Christians high and low. 'They watch over the humble as well as the great and the ignorant and the penitent sinner as well as the holy. There is not a Christian in the whole world who is living in God's faith and fear but is under the protection of the strong and holy angels,' as scripture shows.

In a lengthy conclusion Newman draws from the account of the angels the lesson of humility. 'If Angels who excel in strength, attend upon us, how ready should we be to serve one another—if Angels whose holiness is so bright and dazzling condescend to guard, guide, watch over, comfort, and support us sinners, how should we not be ready in turn to humble ourselves to the lowest of our brethren, who are one nature with us, to bring up children (1 Tim. 5), to lodge strangers, to wash the Saints' feet, to relieve the afflicted, to follow diligently every good work. Blessed lot indeed, if it be given us, to make ourselves the servants of all. This is the lesson taught us by the condescension of the Holy Angels.'

In words as applicable today as in Newman's day, he remarks, 'I think we must allow that we do not make so much of the Holy Angels as we should, in our religion.' Men of the world, he says, do not feel the need of this gracious revelation; they depend on each other, but 'those who follow God need some fellowship which this world cannot give. They have few on earth . . . to take their part—and they look out of this world for comfort and support. *They* feel the graciousness of that revelation we this day commemorate. They feel that God has compassioned them, in introducing them into a heavenly society while taking them from an earthly. He had bid us give up this world, but He has given us another. He has brought us into the kingdom of heaven. The kingdom of heaven is not empty. It is filled with Saints and Angels. We see them not—but let us have faith and we shall enjoy them.'

Catechetical Instruction on the Angels

As has been said, Newman believed that sermons were not enough to teach Christian doctrine; they need to be supplemented by catechesis. Spending the Lent of 1840 at Littlemore, he catechized the children there. As J. B. Mozley wrote his sister, 'Newman's catechising has been a great attraction this Lent, and men have gone out of Oxford every Sunday to hear it. I heard him last Sunday, and thought it very striking: done with such spirit, and the children so up to it; answering with the greatest alacrity. It would have provoked some people's bile immoderately to have heard them all unanimous on the point of the nine orders of angels; the definiteness of the number being in itself a great charm to the minds of the children.' It is revealing that Newman always asked where the children knew the answer to his question, and they had to cite the place in Scripture.

As a Catholic Newman continued to include the angels in his catechetical instructions. There is but one set of notes for a single lecture in

1849, but in September 1860 he spent four Sundays on them, giving a much fuller account. He began the first lecture by remarking that the angels were created from the beginning of all things, when God created the heavens and them *in* heaven. By comparison with men they are pure spirits, and consequently not shackled by bodies as man who is spirit but in a body. 'Hence we are *sluggish, passionate,* etc. we *sleep,* not they—We cannot move about quickly; they in the twinkling of an eye move from heaven to earth.' The angels are the most perfect of all creatures, 'the image of God's attributes,' a statement which Newman unfortunately does not develop in his notes. Unlike men the angels do not *learn,* they do not discover, but intuit all things of the world, in comparison of which the knowledge of the greatest philosophers (among whom Newman would place scientists) is indeed very little. They know God and His attributes, and see God in all things, not being seduced by the creature.

The angels love God above all things, and each other and each order of angels, in its own degree, fittingly. Nevertheless, there are three points which they do not have by nature: (1) knowledge of the future; (2) knowledge of the heart; and (3) knowledge of the mysteries of grace. By way of conclusion Newman spoke of all the wonderful things in creation and how in comparison an angel is more wonderful than all, and if a creature is so wonderful, what must its Creator be? (*SN,* pp. 161–63)

In his second lecture Newman asserted that we know of only one other world besides the present visible one and that is the world of the angels, though there may be other worlds we know not of. The angelic world differs from the visible one in that 'each part is perfect and independent of any other part.' Despite differences, *all* angels excel in two things, namely, strength and purity, in support of which statement he quotes various Scripture texts. For example, regarding their purity, because they have no bodies, he mentions that 'In the resurrection they shall neither marry, nor be married, but shall be as the angels in heaven.' (Matt. 22:30) The strength of the angels is testified to in the Old Testament, as has been said, for example, Exod. 12; 2 Kings 24; 4 Kings 19. As to their number there are guardian angels everywhere, one to every man, though at one time a thousand millions of men. As to their differences, Newman says that some hold the opinion that they differ from each other specifically, that is, each is a species in itself 'as eagle, dove and nightingale.' This is the opinion of St Thomas. Newman says that he himself has never been able to think of them in any other way, since they are pure spirits, and there are no parts or wholes in the angelical world.

Leaving aside this question he proceeds to enumerate the nine orders of angels in three hierarchies:

1st Hierarchy—Seraphim, Cherubim, Thrones
2nd Hierarchy—Dominations, Virtues, Powers
3rd Hierarchy—Principalities, Archangels, Angels

This enumeration is taken from the Pseudo-Dionysius (the original proponent of them) but via Petavius and Bail, to whom Newman refers. (SN, p. 340, n. 13)

Newman then passes on from a consideration of the angels in their nature to what they are by grace, and he affirms that from the first instant of their creation they were endowed with grace, that is, habitual grace, 'with the virtues of faith, hope, charity, a knowledge of the Holy Trinity, etc.' The 'etc.' indicates that he must have mentioned other doctrines of which they have knowledge. While all the angels are holy, having all the virtues, still in proportion to their nature, each ascending order has not only all virtues in greater perfection, but a characteristic virtue as well. These he enumerates as follows:

1) Angels—contentment
2) Archangels—imitation of the perfection of all the other orders; absence of pride and rivalry
3) Principalities—simplicity of intention
4) Powers—tenderness and sweetness
5) Virtues—courage
6) Dominations—zeal
7) Thrones—submission and resignation
8) Cherubim—knowledge
9) Seraphim—love

As to the honor due to the angels, Newman cites passages from the Old Testament where figures such as Joshua and Gideon paid reverence to the angels they encountered, for example, Exodus 23; Joshua 5; Judges 6, 12; Daniel 10. He then explained Revelation 19:10, where despite their greatness St John is told not to adore them. In conclusion Newman remarked 'Let us honour them in the best way, but imitating, like the archangels, the virtues of each order.' (*SN*, pp. 163–64)

The Fallen Angels

In his third lecture Newman took up the subject of the fallen angels. And he began by saying that all the angels were created perfect and gifted with supernatural holiness, even Lucifer, but all of them were put on trial. They did not see God. The length of the trial is difficult to determine, shorter than man's because of their supernatural nature, but Newman queries in a parenthesis why not in an instant? To the question who fell, he replies, some out of all the orders and Lucifer was a seraph. As to the numbers who fell some think it a third by reason of Revelation 13:4. The sin of the angels was one and the same in all from imitation, but they were led by Lucifer. The nature of their sin was all in one, but doubtless it was especially the sin of pride. What *kind* of pride? Obstinacy, ambition, disobedience, arrogance?—all types, but especially reliance on and contentment in *natural* gifts, while despising *supernatural* ones. In addition to pride there was a sort of *sensual* love of self; presumption, ambition, hatred of God; and jealousy of man who was to be created.

Newman then went on to talk of the battle in heaven between the two sides, the good angels led by Michael, with the result that the evil angels were cast into hell. One would like to know how Newman developed the following note: 'Cast into hell—fire in their spirit—though they are now out of it [till the day of judgment].' An interesting conclusion was devoted to a comparison with matters in Italy, presumably the struggle over the temporal power of the Pope. Newman remarks, 'Good and bad not so keenly divided as in angels, but still it is the devil against Michael.' (*SN*, pp. 165–66)

The Guardian Angels

The final lecture was devoted to the guardian angels. Each of the angels has a different work. The Greek word *aggelos* denotes work or service.

Asking the question which order of angels has to do with the visible universe, Newman replies that the lowest, that is, the *angels* are the ministers. Mundane or exterior, and heavenly or domestic works are performed by the angels. But there are extraordinary missions such as that of the Cherubim of Eden (Gen. 3:24); the Seraph in Isaiah (6:6) purifying the prophet's lips with living coal from the altar; Gabriel and Mary in the Annunciation. He mentions one angel giving a charge to another, but gives no scriptural reference.

The first work of the angels with regard to the universe is directing the motion of the heavenly bodies, a patristic idea he developed in the published sermon, 'The Powers of Nature,' as has been noted. The second work of the angels is to act as guardians of nations, provinces, cities, bishoprics, and churches. As to individuals, every one has a guardian angel from the time of the soul's creation until death, and this includes Judas and Antichrist. (*SN,* pp. 166–67)

Newman's most imaginative presentation of the role of the guardian angels is presented in the dialogue between Gerontius and his guardian angel in the *Dream of Gerontius* while the angels sing the praises of God, beginning with 'Praise to the Holiest in the height and in the depth be praise,' which was so memorably scored by Elgar in his *Oratorio.* Newman once summed up in a passing remark what we know of the angels, that 'they say Holy, Holy, Holy, and that they do God's bidding. Worship and service make up their blessedness; and such is our blessedness in proportion as we approach them.' (*PPS* VIII, 18, pp. 264–65)

Note

1. From the Fathers of the Church Newman was aware that the appearances of angels in the Old Testament were variously interpreted: 'Elsewhere Athan. says that "the Angel who delivered Jacob from all evil" from whom he asked a blessing, was not a created Angel, but the Angel of great Counsel, the Word of God Himself, Orat. iii. §12; but he says shortly afterwards that the Angel that appeared to Moses in the Bush "was not the God of Abraham, but what was seen was an Angel, and in the Angel God spoke," §14.' (*Ath.* II, 11.)

Later Newman wrote, 'In the Old Testament, the angel sometimes appears by himself as a messenger from God and then receives homage as such; sometimes he is the manifestation of a Divine Presence and thus becomes relatively an object of worship. The angel in Judg. ii, 1, was a messenger, so was the angel in Dan. x. 5; but the angels in Exod. III, 2, Acts vii. 30, Josh. v. 13, Judg. vi. 11 and xiii 3, were the attendants upon God. In the last three passages the manifestation is first of the angel, then of the Lord of angels. First it was an angel that appeared to Gideon, then "the Lord *looked upon* him," on which, recognizing the divine Presence, he offered sacrifice. So Joshua first addressed the angel, but the words "Loose thy shoes," &c., told him who was there.' (*VM* II, 112, n. 1)

Chapter Ten

Communication with the Invisible World: Prayer

NEWMAN REMARKS in one sermon that our intercourse with our fellow-men is maintained not by sight, but by sound, not by eyes, but by ears. So it is with the Christian 'whose conversation is in heaven.' The primary means of communicating with the inhabitants of the invisible world is through prayer. Nevertheless, Newman's views on prayer underwent a development from his early days as an Evangelical.

One of his earliest sermons—the fifth—was devoted to the importance of prayer.[1] The greater part of it is taken up with a discussion of the proper dispositions for prayer, namely, a recognition of our need for God's grace and help, sinners that we are, and a desire for these gifts, especially holiness. Implied in these dispositions is a recognition of one's dependence upon the Being to whom we pray and also an expectation that God will provide help. These dispositions likewise include a belief in divine providence, since one cannot think of God as able and willing to help us 'while we attribute the course of events merely to chance, necessity, or human contrivance, and exclude "the immediate operation of the First Cause,"' the latter statement being a quotation from Thomas Scott.[2] Although Newman does not develop it in this sermon, the concept of God's providence both general and particular was integral to his thinking about prayer. He came to see as a great mystery how God's will is realized despite the free decisions of men which are often contrary to it, and how prayer may be said to influence God.[3]

In this sermon too Newman makes the usually sharp evangelical distinction between the 'spiritual,' 'religious,' or 'real' Christian, and the worldly man who has no consciousness of his need for help and hence no desire, no taste for religion. How can such a man as the latter pray feelingly, he asks. The importance of proper feelings and affections is thus assumed in Newman's discussion. In the sermon, Newman makes use of two rather plain and unexciting metaphors. What he meant by them, however, is theologically significant. Prayer is said to be the breath and pulse of the spiritual life. What did he mean by these metaphors? As he explained, unless we breathe we die, and so unless our souls receive continued support from the Spirit of God, that is, the Holy Ghost, 'all heavenly affections will languish, droop and ultimately at length perish.' Newman therefore recommends that we pray in or by the Spirit, especially invoking him at the beginning of our prayer. Scripture teaches, he says, that though we know not what to pray for, the Spirit makes intercession for us with groanings that cannot be uttered or put into words (Rom. 8:26). Hence our first petition in prayer should be for heavenly aid to know what things to ask of God.

Second, prayer is said to be the pulse of the spiritual life. From it we may gauge whether the soul is in good health or not. And so 'if we find ourselves cold and careless in prayer, or irregular, or hurried, or inattentive, we should seriously ask ourselves . . . whether something has not disagreed, so to say, with our souls—whether some worldly object is not leading our thoughts from religion.' Worldliness for the Evangelicals was the great obstacle to holiness. Now since, as Newman insists in sermon upon sermon, the Christian is called to holiness in this life to prepare himself for the afterlife, prayer obviously assumes great importance, so that Newman can rightly deduce that there is a reciprocal relation between the spirit of prayer and a holy life—'the more we pray, the holier will be our life; and the holier our life, the more we shall pray.' One further recommendation is offered by way of conclusion to this sermon: as we should begin in the Spirit, so also we should conclude our prayers through Christ, since he is the only mediator between God and man (1 Tim. 2), the only advocate we have with the Father (1 John 20); he is our great High Priest (Heb. 4), and we must come to the Father in the merits of his Son and his name (John 14). The trinitarian orientation of Newman's teaching on prayer is clearly evident here. Faith in the Trinity was, he said in the *Apologia,* first planted deep in his mind by the writings of Thomas Scott, to whom he owed much of what he had to say in this sermon.[4]

We may look at one other sermon on prayer and various occasional statements on prayer in the St Clement's sermons. They deal for the most part with the objects for which one prays, emphasis being placed on the primacy of spiritual rather than temporal benefits, the latter being prayed for only conditionally.[5] It is well to note, however, that Newman's understanding of the Church was beginning to be enlarged during this period, especially with reference to its visible aspects.[6] This and an increasing sacramental understanding of grace enlarged and deepened Newman's doctrine of prayer, which perforce must now include public as well as private prayer. In 1829–30 Newman preached a number of sermons on private and public prayer at St Mary's, Oxford. By this time he no longer considered himself an Evangelical, a fact that is reflected both in his remarks on the role of emotions in prayer and in his sacramental understanding of public and private prayer.

Habitual Prayer or Prayer of the Presence of God

Preaching on the text 'Pray without ceasing' (1 Thess. 5:17), Newman described a type of prayer which might be called living in the presence of God, and this can be done at all times and in any place.[7] At first he says this prayer is commanded as a duty, but modifies this to 'rather it is a characteristic, of those who are really servants and friends of Christ.' In fact, he goes on to establish that it is both a dictate of conscience as well as a mark of the true Christian. To be truly religious is to have this habit of continual prayer. The new life of a Christian is a life of faith, and what is faith, Newman asks, 'but the looking to God and thinking of him continually, holding habitual fellowship with him, that is, speaking to him in our hearts all through the day, praying without ceasing?' From Newman's description of this type of prayer, it is evident that it is not at all times expressed in words. It is, for example, 'doing all things to God's glory; that is, so placing God's presence and will before us, and so consistently acting with a reference to Him, that all we do becomes one body and course of obedience, witnessing without ceasing to Him who made us, and whose servants we are.' It is, in short, 'living in God's sight.'

Many years later Newman enlarged on this idea, calling it meditation on Christ. 'It is to have Him before our minds as One whom we may contemplate, worship, and address when we rise up, when we lie down, when we eat and drink, when we are at home and abroad, when we are working, or walking, or at rest, when we are alone, and again when we are in company; this is meditating . . . and this even the most unlearned person can do, and will do, if he has a will to do it.' (*PPS* VI, 4, pp. 41–42)

The continuity of the former sermon with those delivered at St Clement's may be observed by Newman's reaffirmation that prayer is the breath and pulse of the spiritual life within us, the new life implanted by the Holy Spirit. But Newman also observes that the ordinary Christian has little prayer life; he prays only now and then, when he needs something or when his feelings are unusually excited. His religious life depends on accidental excitement, which Newman is now prepared to declare 'is no test of a religious heart.' This note of distrust of religious emotion is one that appears frequently in subsequent sermons, and it is the issue on which he is most actively opposed to the Evangelicals. The reason for this distrust was the conviction based upon personal experience that a concentration and preoccupation with feeling turn one's attention to one's self, culminating in a dangerous introspection and contemplation of one's feelings rather than centering one's attention on the object of one's faith, namely, Christ.[8]

Times of Private Prayer

One would perhaps conclude that, having proclaimed the importance of constant and habitual prayer, Newman was indifferent whether one set aside fixed times for formal prayer. On the contrary, he declared that it is highly expedient to have such set times and forms even for private prayer, and indeed such times are commanded in Scripture.[9] The chief reason assigned for stated times of prayer, especially morning and evening, is that without them formal prayer at other times and habitual prayer during the day are unlikely to be maintained. Morning and evening prayer help create regularity in our spiritual life, whereas 'he who gives up regularity in prayer has lost a principal means of reminding himself that the spiritual life is obedience to a Lawgiver, not a mere feeling or a taste.'

Forms of Private Prayer

In addition to set times for prayer Newman recommended the use of set forms as well. [10] His reasons were connected with his strong opposition to ex tempore prayers, which he thought irreverent because they were expressed in unsuitable language and involved 'rude, half-religious thoughts.' Set forms of prayer also guarded, he believed, against two other forms of irreverence: distracted and wandering thoughts on the one hand, and excited thoughts on the other. The Dissenters and the Evangelicals at times criticized set forms of prayer as creating a cold formalism. With them in mind, though not explicitly mentioning them, Newman declared that forms of prayer 'are censured for the very circumstances about them which is their excellence. They are accused of impeding the current of devotion, when, in fact, that (so-called) current is in itself faulty, and ought to be checked.' While admitting that on occasion emotions will break through forms of prayer, he nevertheless maintained that this should not be the ordinary course, and attacked the belief that feelings are an indication of earnestness in religion. On the contrary, the very purpose of fixed forms of prayer is 'to still emotion, to calm us, to remind us what and where we are, to lead us to a purer and serener temper, and to that deep unruffled love of God and man, which is really the fulfilling of the law and the perfection of human nature.' Lastly, Newman saw several other advantages in fixed forms of prayer. They helped one recollect oneself quickly, and they remained in the memory, building around them associations which could prove an aid in time of temptation, perhaps even to be recalled when one fell into sin.

Public Worship

In a sermon preached on 25 October 1829, Newman raised the question frequently asked by young people today: Why go to church? They usually do not proceed further to Newman's second question: Why is it not sufficient to pray in private?[11] Newman's answers to these questions are basically ecclesiological. Christ has lodged his blessings in a body or Church, which exists before the individual is admitted into it, which does not depend on the individual member, but the individual member depends on the body. Newman appeals to St Paul and the apostles who speak of Christians as forming one body, praying together, sanctified together as one temple of Christ and his Holy Spirit. He also cites the text of his sermon, 'where two or three are gathered together in my name, there am I in the midst of them.' Since the Church mediates and applies the blessings of Christ to the individual, who is admitted into the body by the social and external rite of baptism, public prayer has preceded private. Indeed from this public adoption and gift of grace, private prayer takes its value. On the basis of this sacramental view of the Church, therefore, Newman can affirm that the Christian's hope of an answer to his private prayer arises from his having also prayed in public.

In addition to Baptism, the Eucharist is also a channel of grace, and these sacraments (except in case of necessity) are performed publicly in church. The other ordinances set down in the Book of Common Prayer are likewise administered in church: confirmation, marriage, thanksgivings, and burials, even if not necessary for salvation, as are baptism and communion, according to Anglican teaching. If public prayer is so essential, why do we come to church just once a week? Newman replies that the Lord's day is a most appropriate one and set down in Scripture, but there is no reason for limiting it to that day. He adds: 'the blessing promised on meeting together naturally leads thoughtful men to wish to meet more frequently.' He quotes most appropriately Psalm 84: 'how amiable are Thy tabernacles, O Lord. . . . My soul longeth, yea, even fainteth for the courts of the Lord—my heart and my flesh crieth out for the living God'.

It may seem incredible to us today, but many people came to church primarily attracted by the sermon or would go from church to church to listen to a preacher of some reputation. Moreover, in rural parishes the clergyman had assumed many functions—doctor, lawyer, magistrate, as well as teacher. As R. W. Church pointed out, 'the idea of the priest was not quite forgotten, but there was much . . . to obscure it.'[12] It is against this background that one must place Newman's assertion that the primary function of a Christian minister is his priestly function and he is a priest in church precisely 'as offering up the sacrifice of prayer and praise from the whole congregation, binding together the worship of individuals into that one united voice to which the christian blessings are distinctly pledged.'[13] This he does through the mediation of Christ. Second, the priest commemorates in the sacrament of the Lord's Supper the one perfect and sufficient sacrifice which Christ made on the cross. As is clear from the rest of the sermon, Newman at this point of his development is not prepared, though he may be later, to look upon the Eucharist as a sacrifice.[14] There is, however, not merely a commemorative significance to his action, but an eschatological one, for the priest prepares the faithful for their final consecration to God at the last day.[15] Although the time of public service is a most suitable one to hear a sermon, the latter 'is far inferior in dignity to the prayers, and it is for the sake of them, and is not necessary to divine worship which is complete without it.'[16]

The Psalms, the Prayer of the Church

Writing to Henry Wilberforce in March 1837 in answer to questions a lady enquirer had put regarding prayer, Newman replied, 'The Psalms should be the basis of all devotion. . . . This is one great excellence of the Psalms—as being not *continual addresses* to Almighty God, (which require a great effort and stretch of mind) but meditations on His attributes etc. mutual exhortations, interspersed with some more like prayers.'[17] He later published a sermon on the Psalms, in which he affirmed that they have a meaning for all times. Many of the Psalms relate to our Lord Jesus Christ. Moreover, the Church has appropriated the Psalms because she is holy and defenseless. And from beginning to end the Psalter is a supplication to God to rescue the poor and needy, and to justify the righteous.

The Psalms contain two main ideas: the defeat of God's enemies and the suffering of God's people. Consequently, when we pray the Psalms we are triumphing in the exultation of the Church over the world in so far as the world separates itself from God. And as the Church is always persecuted, it appeals to God for help and protection. The second great and more frequent theme is the suffering of God's people, and God's creative and redemptive love for them. To the new people of God, Christ's Church, they speak of that love in its fullest manifestation.

The individual who prays the Psalms identifies himself with the Church and prays in her name. To the objection that a particular local Church is not persecuted, and therefore using the language of the Psalms is unreal, Newman replied that some part of the Body is always suffering, and since 'we are members of the *one* body of Christ, we must feel for the rest, in whatever part of the world they are, when they are persecuted, and must remember them in our prayers.' (*SD,* sermon 18)

As a Catholic Newman made the same recommendation to a spiritual enquirer that the Psalms be made the basis of prayer. He himself loved the breviary, particularly the Sunday office because it was longer than the other offices.

Intercessory Prayer

Perhaps the most characteristic aspect of Newman's teaching on prayer is the special role he assigns to intercessory prayer.[18] Basing his teaching on St Paul's Epistles and the Acts of the Apostles, Newman concluded that 'intercession is the characteristic of Christian worship, the privilege of the heavenly adoption, the exercise of the perfect and spiritual mind.' It is especially the prerogative and privilege of the obedient and the holy. Behind Newman's concept of intercessory prayer is the theology of the Holy Spirit. By the time he wrote the sermon on this topic, he had come under the influence of the Greek Fathers, particularly St Athanasius, and adopted their doctrine of the indwelling of the Holy Spirit, conferred in baptism and elevating the Christian to a supernatural plane.[19] The Holy Spirit unites the baptized not only with Christ, but, as he had come to believe while still an Evangelical, with each other.[20] Under the inspiration of the Holy Spirit, the Christian is made over into the image of Christ, so that as Christ intercedes above, the Christian intercedes here below. Moreover, when he reads the Scriptures, he is able to see the course of God's providence in the great contest taking place between good and evil, and that by his prayers or absence of them the Christian is involved in an eternal destiny. In the contest between good and evil the Christian by reason of his intercessory power plays a role. On the one hand Newman calls this 'O mystery of blessedness too great to think of steadily, lest we grow dizzy.' On the other hand he is overwhelmed by the responsibility one has of interceding for others. 'How can we answer to ourselves for the souls . . . that have been lost . . . seeing that, for what we know, we were ordained to influence or reverse their present destiny and have not done it?'

Newman's Practice of Prayer as an Anglican

We know that Newman composed long lists of petitions that he prayed for each morning and night, varying them from day to day.[21] There is a record of his bidding prayers at St Mary's, which is quite extensive. Also extant are long lists of names of those for whom he prayed, including almost everyone connected with the Oxford Movement. In this as in other aspects of his teaching on prayer, Newman practiced what he preached, or perhaps it is more accurate to say that he preached what he practiced. There are prayers that he composed for morning and night, written in 1817, 1818, 1824, and 1828. These morning and evening prayers are really a combination of meditation and petition. The meditations on Christian doctrine in the latter part of *Meditations and Devotions* give an idea of what they are like. Petitions were composed in 1824–25, further prayers in 1837 and thereafter. Possibly others existed but were destroyed. We know from his journals that he prayed constantly on walks and in business.[22] Furthermore, he introduced the daily service at St Mary's on 14 October 1834, preaching on its importance on 2 November 1834.[23] He wrote tracts on the liturgy, particularly on the breviary as part of the corporate worship of the Church.[24] He prayed privately for the dead, though he did not introduce it aloud into the liturgy, because he thought it might be falsely linked with the Roman doctrine of purgatory.[25] His life at Littlemore may be characterized as a life of continual prayer. In saying the breviary, while an Anglican, however, Newman omitted the invocations addressed to Our Lady.[26]

Newman's Doctrine and Practice of Prayer as a Catholic

Upon becoming a Catholic, Newman of course believed in the invocation to Our Lady and of the saints, the seven sacraments, the sacrifice of the mass, and the doctrine of purgatory as taught by the Catholic Church. Allowance being made for these changes, there is still a marked continuity between Newman's teaching and practice of prayer as an Anglican and as a Catholic. How strong Newman's belief in the efficacy of prayer remained may be judged from a letter written 28 February 1876 to William Philip Gordon:

> I have said three Masses for your intention concerning your brother. I can but repeat, that it is a thought I have made much use of for more than fifty years, that, so great is the power of prayer and the promise made to it, that I believe it to be successful in a particular case, though there be nothing in the visible disposition of things to countenance that belief, or when, rather, sight is in opposition to that belief.[27]

In his letters to enquirers who were attracted to the Catholic Church but unable to take the step of joining it, he regularly recommended that they pray earnestly for light and grace.[28] In his letter to Pusey he reaffirmed his belief that 'prayer is the very essence of all religion' and that intercessory prayer whose vital force stems from sanctity is a 'first principle of the Church's life' and that the Spirit of Christ, the Holy Spirit, is the great Intercessor.[29] The intercessory power of the Christian, owing to the meritorious sacrifice of Christ, is, Newman affirmed as a Catholic, most fittingly exercised in the sacrifice of the mass.[30] Needless to say, long lists of persons to be prayed for were read every day before Newman celebrated mass. Above the entrance door to the Oratory Newman had written: Domus mea domus orationis vocabitur.

One aspect of prayer life which was not only added when he became a Catholic but both practiced and recommended to others, was devotion to Christ reserved in the Blessed Sacrament. In the sorrow and loneliness of his first years as a Catholic, his greatest cross was being cut off from his family and friends in the Anglican Church.[31] On a number of occasions he mentions it in his letters and also remarks that living in a house with the Blessed Sacrament which he could visit was an enormous consolation and strength in this trial.[32] In Dublin he received permission from Dr Cullen to have reservation in a private chapel.[33] Before exposing the ex-Dominican friar, Achilli, as a profligate in one of his 'Lectures on the Present Position of Catholics in England,' he 'went before the Blessed

Sacrament and begged to be kept from doing it, if wrong.'[34] When the trial for libel lasting four days was in process, Newman spent almost night and day before It in the London oratory, thereby leaving an indelible impression on his fellow Oratorians.[35] Of a chapel of reservation he once wrote, 'It is the place for intercession surely.'[36] To Lady Chatterton he remarked, 'there is no benediction from earth or sky which falls upon us like that which comes to us from the Blessed Sacrament, which is Himself.'[37] He often recommended this devotion to converts suffering from solitariness.[38]

Notes

1. MS sermon no. 5, 'Prayer.'

2. Thomas Scott, 'On Prayer,' in *Essays on the most important subjects in Religion,* 7th ed., London 1814, p. 380. All unpublished MS sermons of Newman are in the Oratory Archives, Birmingham.

3. See *PPS* VI, sermon 17, pp. 247–50. Also, 'A Particular Providence as revealed in the Gospel,' *PPS* III, sermon 9; MS sermon no. 14: 'it [prayer] sets vibrating (as it were) the whole system and series of God's providence and gracious dispensations to mankind; it exerts its influence over ages yet unborn, and is felt at the very ends of the earth.' 'So again, when men who profess Christianity ask how prayer can really influence the course of God's Providence they rationalize . . . the idea of Mystery is discarded.' ('On the Introduction of rationalistic principles into Revealed Religion,' *Ess.* I, pp. 33–34)

4. MS sermon no. 5. Scott, *op. cit.,* pp. 378–93.

5. MS sermon no. 14. See MS sermon no. 150: Since Christ does not pledge himself to give temporal blessings as these were promised to the Jews, may 'God enable us never to pray for worldly blessings but with the addition "Thy will be done,"—but with the limitation "if O Lord it will not interfere with our *spiritual* interests."' Also MS sermons no. 67, no. 103 *passim.*

6. 'He has bound the Church together in one visible union and fellowship. He has appointed a certain ordinance for admission into the Redeemer's Kingdom—even that of baptism. He has bid us, in remembrance of him, meet to eat of one bread and drink of one cup. He has sanctioned our meeting together at stated times to offer prayer and praise with one voice. . . . In a word he has appointed a visible body of a Church.' (MS sermon no. 121, 'On the use of the Visible Church')

7. 'Mental Prayer,' preached on 13 December 1829, *PPS* VII, sermon 15. Quotations are from pp. 204, 209–10, 206, 207.

8. 'Self-contemplation,' *PPS* II, sermon 15. Cf. 'Religious Worship a Remedy for Excitements,' *PPS* III, sermon 23, and *Jfc.,* p. 330. See *AW,* pp. 179, 82, for the warning Newman's father gave him.

9. 'Times of Private Prayer,' preached 20 December 1829, *PPS* I, sermon 19.

10. 'Forms of Private Prayer,' originally joined with 'Times of Private Prayer' and preached on the same day, *PPS* I, sermon 20.

11. MS sermon no. 213: 'On the Duty of Public Worship,' preached on 25 October 1829.

12. R. W. Church, *The Oxford Movement: Twelve Years 1833–1845,* London 1900, p. 4.

13. MS sermon no. 224: 'The Liturgy, the Service of the Christian Priest,' preached on 31 January 1830 and repeated on 7 October 1832 according to the diary for that day.

14. Especially the remarks about the Roman Catholics having 'made the Lord's supper a literal sacrifice to God—and they suppose Christ's blessed body actually to be present on a real altar—and the priest offers it up, as the Jewish priest offered *his* sacrifices.' (p. 23) See, however, *Jfc.,* pp. 198–201.

15. 'And you meet together in this place of worship at set times . . . and to prefigure that final consecration of yourself as His at the last day, when once for all and for ever He who has now begun the good work in you will stablish your hearts unblameable in holiness before His Father at His coming with all His Saints.' (p. 29)

16. MS sermon no. 214, fragment on preaching, preached on 1 November 1829; MS sermon no. 290: 'On the Object and Effects of Preaching,' first preached on 20 March 1831: 'It is the peculiar office of *public prayer* to bring down Christ among us; it is as being many collected into one, that Christ recognizes us as His. And this, then, is the great reason of our meeting together in Christ for common prayer.'

17. N to H. W. Wilberforce, 25 March 1837, *LD* VI, 47.

18. 'Intercession,' *PPS* III, sermon 24, preached 22 February 1835.

19. 'The Incarnation,' *PPS* II, sermon 3, pp. 34–35, preached on 25 December 1834; 'The Indwelling Spirit,' *PPS* II, sermon 19 (1834).

20. 'We must not consider the Holy Spirit as uniting us only to Him; the same Divine Agent, also unites us one to another.' (MS sermon no. 120, 'On the Communion of Saints,' preached 27 November 1825)

21. BOA, A.10.4.

22. *AW,* p. 205. Cf also p. 246.

23. *LD* IV, 339, 351.

24. Tracts 3, 75, 88.

25. *LD* V, 305; cf. pp. 260, 303.

26. F. W. Faber to JHN, 28 November 1844, and JHN to F. W. Faber, 1 December 1844. *KC,* pp. 356–57.

27. *LD* XXVIII, 34. Cf. *MD,* pp. 70–71.

28. As examples, see letters to A. J. Hanmer, 10 February 1848, *LD* XII, 168; to Mrs William Froude, 2 March 1854, *LD* XVI, 66; to Louisa Simeon, 25 June 1869, *LD* XXIV, 276.

29. 'Letter to Rev E. B. Pusey, D.D.,' *Diff.* II, 68–71.

30. *Sermon Notes,* 2d ed., London 1914, pp. 192–93.

31. 'My severance from him (Rogers) and others is a wound which will never heal.' To William Froude, 2 January 1860, *LD* XIX, 273.

32. To Mrs J. W. Bowden, 1 March 1846, *LD* XI, pp. 130–31; To W. J. Copeland, 10 March 1846, *LD* XI, p. 133.

33. To Archbishop Cullen, 8 December 1854, *LD* XVI, 320; 24 January 1855, *LD* XVI, p. 358.

34. To Richard Stanton, 4 December 1851, *LD* XIV, 451.

35. Among notes of Events, preserved at the London Oratory, under the year 1852: 'Dr Newman stayed in King William Street during the course of the Achilli trial in the Court of Queen's Bench. He spent almost day and night before the Tabernacle, and his serenity and calmness in the midst of the excitement without were remarkable.' (*LD* XV, 104, n. 2)

36. To H. W. Wilberforce, 26 February 1846, *LD* XI, 129.

37. To Lady Chatterton, Holy Thursday 1866, LD XXII, 194.

38. To Helen Douglas Forbes, 4 October 1864, *LD* XXI, 249.

IV   Patterns of Holiness

Chapter Eleven

Christ, the Pattern of the Christian Life

To be a Christian is to follow Christ. He is the leader, model, and pattern of all Christian behavior and development. 'He who is the first principle and pattern of all things, came to be the beginning and pattern of human kind, the first-born of the whole Creation.' And so He is 'a pattern of sanctity in the circumstances of His life.' (*PPS* V, 7, p. 93) Newman attempted to delineate the Christian character which is patterned after Christ, but by character he meant not in the psychological but rather in the theological or moral sense. One way of approaching the subject was not to describe the character itself, but to enumerate the maxims of Christian morality which are intended to form such a character as these maxims are revealed in various scriptural precepts:

> Such are the following passages—we are bid not to resist evil, but to turn the cheek to the smiter; to forgive from our hearts our brother, though he sin against us until seventy times seven; to love and bless our enemies; to love without dissimulation; to esteem others better than ourselves; to bear one another's burdens; to condescend to men of low estate; to minister to our brethren the more humbly, the higher our station is; to be like little children in simplicity and humility. We are to guard against every idle word, and to aim at great plainness of speech; to make prayer our solace, and hymns and psalms our mirth; to be careless about the honours and emoluments of the world; to maintain almost a voluntary poverty (at least so far as renouncing all superfluous wealth may be called such); to observe a purity severe as an utter abhorrence of uncleanness can make it to be; willingly to part with hand or eye in the desire to be made like to the pattern of the Son of God; and to think little of friends or country, or the prospects of ordinary domestic happiness, for the kingdom of heaven's sake.

If we look at how this morality formed the saints after the model of Christ we see that there is a combination of graces, indicating that moral growth is symmetrical. St Paul, for example, exhibits the union of zeal and gentleness, St John, of overflowing love and uncompromising strictness of principle. These are examples of the *coincidentia oppositorum* already spoken of: love and fear of God, use of the world without its abuse, to which might be added self-respect and humility. Some of these are the perfection of natural virtue, others go beyond it. (*OUS,* sermon 3) For example, Christ showed us how to love and care for our relatives and friends and thereby extend our love further and further to others and how to sympathize with others in times of sorrow. Yet like Him we must be ready 'to hate' them according to His injunction, 'he that loveth father and mother more than Me, is not worthy of Me,' that is, 'we may be called upon to forget them in pursuit of higher duties.' (*PPS* II, sermon 5; III, sermon 10)

All attempts to follow Christ will involve self-denial in accordance with Christ's injunction, 'If any man will come after Me, let him deny himself, and take up his cross daily and follow me.' Consequently, efforts at Christian obedience are not occasional but regular. They do not necessarily involve heroic deeds. Daily self-denial 'consists in the continual practice of small duties which are distasteful to us.' Every person has a weakness of some sort. One is passionate or ill-tempered, another vain, another with little control over his tongue. By resisting one's weakness, one strengthens one's general power of self-mastery, so that if one is taken off-guard only at times, for example in experiencing passion or anger, one will gradually get mastery of it. (*PPS* I, 5, pp. 67–69)

Such taking on ourselves a cross after Christ's pattern is 'not a mere refraining from sin, for He had no sin, but a giving up what we might lawfully use.' It is not necessary, Newman remarks, to determine exactly which lawful things we should deny ourselves. Like St Paul the Christian should fix his eyes upon Christ, become enamored of 'the splendour and glory of His holiness,' and then strive and pray that this love of holiness be created within our hearts. 'Then acts will follow, such as befit us and our circumstances, in due time, without distressing ourselves to find what they should be.' In brief, one should relinquish what one thinks Christ wants us to relinquish. Lest this seem too vague an injunction, Newman specifies instances of taking up the cross: the daily opportunities which occur of yielding to others, when you need not yield, and of doing unpleasant services, which you might avoid; turning from ambitious thoughts, hating to spend money on oneself, learning to master one's heart, when it would burst forth into vehemence or prolong a barren sorrow, or dissolve into unseasonable tenderness; curbing the tongue, and turning away the eyes, lest one fall into temptation, taking up morning and evening prayer. In this way self-denial becomes natural, and a change occurs gently and imperceptibly. (*PPS* VII, sermon 7)

Men know what sin is by experience, says Newman. 'They do not know what holiness is and they cannot obtain the knowledge of its secret pleasure, till they join themselves truly and heartily to Christ, and devote themselves to His service,—till they "taste," and thereby try. . . . None other than God the Holy Spirit can help us in this matter, by enlightening and changing our hearts.' (*PPS* VII, 14, pp. 198–99) Therefore, Newman urges his listeners to take upon themselves the yoke of Christ.

'Take My yoke upon you, and learn of Me, for I am meek and lowly in heart, and ye shall find rest unto your souls; for My yoke is easy, and My burden is light.' It is an easy yoke, he says, for Christ makes it easy, though it remains a yoke, and therefore irksome. It must be taken as a first principle in religion, Newman asserts, that all of us must come to Christ 'in some sense or other, through things naturally unpleasant to us, whether bodily suffering, pain, subduing our natural inclinations, or sacrifice of our natural wishes.' (*PPS* VII, 8, pp. 105–6) This is why he affirms in another sermon that religion is a weariness to the natural man, and in two other sermons why love of religion requires a new nature, which makes 'Religion Pleasant to the Religious' (*PPS* VI, sermon 2; VII, sermons 13 and 14)

The character to which Christ calls us and for which He has given us a new nature in Him, is described in the Sermon on the Mount. Unlike many spiritual writers or moralists, Newman as an Anglican did not distinguish precepts and counsels. All are called to holiness after the pattern of Christ Himself. The character described in the Sermon on the Mount is one 'who is poor in spirit, meek, pure in heart, merciful, peace-making, penitent, and eager after righteousness.' Such a man is truly a 'mortified man.' This character is not at first attractive or pleasant because it involves change, and that a painful one, in one way or another. It involves suffering, for 'Nothing short of suffering, except in rare cases,

makes us what we should be; gentle instead of harsh, meek instead of
violent, conceding instead of arrogant, lowly instead of proud, pure-
hearted instead of sensual, sensitive of sin instead of carnal.'

Through the grace of the Holy Spirit, the effects of these crosses will
be 'to make us like Him who suffered all pains, physical and moral, sin excepted, in its fulness.' We know what His character was: 'how grave and
subdued His speech, His manner, His acts; what calmness, self-possession,
tenderness, and endurance; how He resisted evil; how He turned His cheek
to the smiter; how He blessed when persecuted; how He resigned Himself
to His God and Father, how He suffered silently, and opened not His
mouth, when accused maliciously.' (*PPS* VII, 8, pp. 110–11)

Such a character the world not only does not imitate; it despises it.
This is how it judges it: 'Such a man is unfit for life. . . . he is cowardly
and narrow-minded, unmanly, feeble, superstitious.' Yet such is the pattern which Christ has given and such the character of the apostles and of
all who have conquered the world. Here Newman returns again, as he
does so often, to the dispositions of those who consider themselves Christians but follow the religion of the day, the religion of the world. He
gives yet another clear and precise statement of its characteristic dispositions: 'To have one's own way, to follow one's own tastes, to please one's
self, to have things to one's mind, not to be thwarted, to indulge in the
comforts of life, to do little for God . . . to be afraid of being too
religious, to dread singularity. . . . This . . . is the sort of character
which the multitude, even of what are called respectable men, exemplify.'
(*PPS* VII, sermon 8)

On the other side, what light does the death of the Eternal Word of
God shed on the meaning of life in this world? 'His cross has put its due
value upon every thing which we see. . . . It has taught us how to live,
how to use this world, what to expect, what to desire, what to hope. It is
the tone into which all the strains of this world's music are ultimately
resolved.' The world on the surface seems made for pleasure and for
happiness, but this is a superficial view. 'The doctrine of the Cross does
but teach . . . the very same lesson which the world teaches to those who
live long in it . . . who know it. The world is sweet to the lips, but
bitter to the taste. It pleases at first, but not at last. It looks gay on the
outside, but evil and misery lie concealed within. . . . If we will not
acknowledge that this world has been made miserable by sin, from the

sight of Him on whom our sins were laid, we shall experience it to be miserable by the recoil of those sins upon ourselves.'

At first the doctrine of the cross startles and perhaps repels, and yet it is a true doctrine. It has to be received by faith in the heart. Far from making the Gospel 'a sad religion,' the doctrine of the cross makes it a joyous one. It only forbids us to begin with enjoyment. Begin with the cross and peace and comfort rises out of the sorrow. 'That cross will lead us to mourning, repentance, humiliation, prayer, fasting; we shall sorrow for our sins, we shall sorrow with Christ's sufferings; but all this sorrow will only issue . . . in a happiness far greater than the enjoyment which the world gives.' And so, Newman concludes, 'They alone are able truly to enjoy this world, who begin with the world unseen. They alone enjoy it, who have first abstained from it. . . . They alone are able to use the world, who have learned not to abuse it; they alone inherit it, who take it as a shadow of the world to come, and who for that world to come relinquish it.' (*PPS* VI, 7, pp. 83–93)

Focusing One's Thoughts on Christ

If we do not pattern our lives more on Christ, it is because we have not made Him the center of our thoughts. We do not meditate on Him. What is meditation? Newman asks in this connection. 'It is simply this, thinking habitually and constantly of Him and of His deeds and sufferings. It is to have Him before our minds as One whom we may contemplate, worship, and address when we rise up, when we lie down, when we eat and drink, when we are at home and abroad, when we are working, or walking, or at rest, when we are alone, and again when we are in company; this is meditating.' The fundamental hindrance to such meditation is our hardness of heart. The latter must be broken up, like ground, dug, watered, tended, and cultivated like a garden. This is not the work of a day. It is difficult at first, and one is unaware of progress even as one progresses; only at certain stages in the process do we become conscious of it, but we do not directly perceive the change itself.

As a model of such meditation Newman presents thoughts on Christ's *poverty*, how He suffered hardships from His birth until His death. As he remarked in another sermon, 'He lived through all stages of man's life up to a perfect man, infancy, childhood, boyhood, youth, maturity, that He might be a pattern of them all.' (*SD*, 5, p. 54) He endured cold, heat, and thirst; his fare was meager and plain. He also encountered contempt, hatred, and persecution. He felt bereavement at the death of His friend Lazarus, and overwhelming fear before He suffered. He experienced betrayal by one of his friends, and denial by another. Newman stresses in his account of Christ's privations that He suffered both in soul and body, and therefore in His *humanity*. How little we appreciate His sufferings, how little we feel for Him, he said. (*PPS* VI, sermon 4)

That it is necessary to acquire such 'tender and eager affection towards Our Lord and Saviour,' which he called 'the *beauty* of holiness,' Newman affirmed in another sermon, 'The Crucifixion.' We are not true followers of Christ unless we have true love of Him, but we cannot love Him unless we feel gratitude to Him, and we cannot feel gratitude to Him unless we feel keenly what He suffered for us. Of course, feeling of itself is not enough; indeed without proper conduct, it is a form of hypocrisy, while right conduct without feeling is an imperfect form of religion. To the question of how one learns to feel pain and anguish at the thought of Christ's sufferings, Newman made the same answer as he did in the previous sermon, 'Christ's Privations,' namely, habitual meditation, and he offered some thoughts on Christ as innocent Victim to arouse such feelings. (*PPS* VII, sermon 10)

Newman concluded the former of these two sermons with the wise admonition not to try to work up feelings artificially. 'Deep feeling is but the natural or necessary attendant on a holy heart. . . . We may meditate upon Christ's sufferings; and by this meditation we *shall* gradually, as time goes on, be brought to these deep feelings. We may pray God to do for us what we cannot do for ourselves, to *make* us feel; to give us the spirit of gratitude, love, reverence, self-abasement, godly fear, repentance, holiness, and lively faith.' (*PPS* VI, 4, p. 52)

That Newman himself grew in such deep feeling can be deduced from his sermons and *Meditations and Devotions*. None of the *Parochial and Plain Sermons* on Christ's sufferings can compare with the imaginative and emotional daring with which he enters into Christ's mental sufferings in the sermon in the later *Discourses to Mixed Congregations*, 'Mental Sufferings of Our Lord in His Passion.'

He sets the stage by two introductory observations. The first is that it is relatively easier to meditate upon Christ's physical sufferings as we are aided by the visual presentation of a crucifix. The second is a detailed psychological analysis of pain, the main points of which can only be mentioned. What makes pain so trying, says Newman, is that it possesses the mind, and hence anything that can distract the mind from it, lessens the pain. Again, what makes pain intolerable is its continuance. 'The memory of the foregoing moments of pain acts upon and (as it were) edges the pain that succeeds.'

Applying these remarks to our Lord, Newman recalls how Christ refused the wine mingled with myrrh when He was crucified. He would have been willing to escape pain, had it been His Father's will, but He was determined to embrace it, because it was. As He said to Peter, 'The chalice which My Father hath given Me, shall I not drink it?' He does not, therefore, try to escape from it or to lessen it. On the contrary, He confronted it 'with an advertance and consciousness, and therefore with a keenness and intensity, and with a unity of perception, which none of us can possibly fathom . . . because His soul was so absolutely in His own power, so simply free from the influence of distractions, so fully directed *upon* the pain, so utterly surrendered, so simply subjected to the sufferings. And thus He may truly be said to have suffered the whole of His passion in every moment of it.'

Christ entered into his mental sufferings in the Garden of Olives with a full deliberate act. He withdrew the consciousness of His own innocence and the anticipation of His triumph. And what did He have to bear? 'the weight of sin . . . the sins of the entire world.' Newman then presents an imaginative vision of sin.

There, then, in that most awful hour, knelt the Saviour of the world, putting off the defences of His divinity . . . opening His arms, baring His breast, sinless as He was, to the assault of His foe. . . . There He knelt, motionless and still, while the vile and horrible fiend clad His spirit in a robe steeped in all that is hateful, and heinous in human crime, which clung close round His heart, and filled His conscience, and found its way into every sense and pore of His mind, and spread over Him a moral leprosy, till He almost felt Himself to be that which He never could be. . . . Are these the hands of the Immaculate Lamb of God, once innocent, but now red with ten thousand barbarous deeds of blood? are these His lips, not uttering prayers, and praise . . . but as if defiled with oaths, and blasphemies, and doctrines of devils? or His eyes, profaned as they are by all the evil visions and idolatrous fascinations for

which men have abandoned their Adorable Creator? And His ears, they
ring with sounds of revelry and of strife; and His heart is frozen with
avarice, and cruelty, and unbelief; and His very memory is laden with
every sin which has been committed since the Fall. . . . It is the long
history of a world, and God alone can bear the load of it. Hopes
blighted, vows broken, lights quenched, warnings scorned, opportunities lost; the innocent betrayed, the young hardened, the penitent
relapsing, the just overcome, the aged failing; the sophistry of misbelief,
the wilfulness of passion, the obduracy of pride, the tyranny of habit, the
canker of remorse . . . the anguish of shame, the pining of disappointment, the sickness of despair; such cruel, such pitiable spectacles, such
heartrending, revolting, detestable, maddening scenes; nay, the haggard
faces, the convulsed lips, the flushed cheek, the dark brow of the willing
slaves of evil, they are all before Him now; they are upon Him and in
Him. They are with Him instead of that ineffable peace which has
inhabited His soul since the moment of His conception. They are upon
Him, they are all but His own; He cries to His Father as if He were the
criminal, not the victim; His agony takes the form of guilt and compunction. He is doing penance, He is making confession, He is exercising contrition with a reality and a virtue infinitely greater than that of all
Saints and penitents together; for He is the One Victim for us all, the
sole satisfaction, the real Penitent, all but the real sinner. . . . He rises
languidly from the earth. . . . He turns, and lo! there is blood upon His
garment and His footprints.

At the end of the sermon Newman allowed himself what he rarely did
in his published writings, an intense outburst of love and affection directed to the Heart of Jesus:

> O Heart of Jesus, all Love, I offer Thee these humble prayers for
> myself, and for all those who unite themselves with me in spirit to adore
> Thee. O holiest Heart of Jesus most lovely, I intend to renew and to offer
> to Thee these acts of adoration and these prayers, for myself a wretched
> sinner, and for all those who are associated with me in Thy adoration,
> through all moments while I breathe, even to the end of my life. I
> recommend to Thee, O my Jesus, Holy Church, Thy dear spouse, and
> our true Mother, all just souls and all poor sinners, the afflicted, the
> dying, and all mankind. Let not Thy blood be shed for them in vain.
> Finally, deign to apply it in relief of the souls in Purgatory, of those in

particular, who have practised in the course of their life this holy devotion of adoring Thee. (*Mix.*, sermon 16)

As a result of sin, suffering is the lot of man in this life. Newman warned his hearers that in itself it has no tendency to make men better; it often makes men worse. Consequently it is no sure test of holiness. Nevertheless, if God steps in bringing pain it is that 'men may be like what Christ was, and may be led to think of Him, not of themselves. He brings them into trouble, that they may be near Him.' Hence, if sufferings are accepted in the spirit and love of Christ, they will transform us interiorly. There is the further result God produces by means of pain, the ability to sympathize and enter into the sufferings of others. 'Taught by our own pain, our own sorrow, nay, by our own sin, we shall have hearts and minds exercised for every service of love towards those who need it.' (*PPS* V, 21, pp. 304, 307–8)

Perhaps the distinctive characteristic of the Christian as an image of Christ is humility. Ancient civilization had no idea of such a virtue, Indeed, 'humiliation immoral,' was a first principle of paganism. Newman saw 'a mysterious connection between real advancement and self-abasement: 'If you minister to the humble and despised, if you feed the hungry, tend the sick, succour the distressed; if you bear with the froward, submit to insult, endure ingratitude, render good for evil, you are, as by a divine charm, getting power over the world and rising among the creatures.' So much so is this that God chooses as his instruments the poor and the despised. 'No condescension *can* be so great as that of our Lord *Himself.* Now the more they abase themselves the more *like* they are to Him; and the more like they are to Him, the greater must be their power with Him.' (*Idea*, pp. 204–5; *Call.*, p. 345; *PPS* VI, 22, pp. 319–20)

In this he saw a law of God's providence, and he marshaled many Scripture texts to prove it (e.g., John 13:13, 17; Luke 14:8, 10, 11; Matt. 5:39; 2 Cor. 12:10; Rom. 12:19–30). Then, bringing the admonitions of St Paul to bear on the common human reaction to humiliations, he asked, 'has a man been insolent to you, shown contempt of you, thwarted you, outwitted you, been cruel to you,—and you feel resentment and your feeling is this, "I wish him no ill, but I would like him just to be brought down for this, and to make amends to me"; rather say, hard though it be, "I will overcome him with love; except severity be a duty, I will say nothing; I will keep quiet, I will seek to do him a service; I owe him a service, not a grudge; and I will be kind, and sweet, and gentle, and composed; and while I cannot disguise from him that I know well where he stands, and where I, still this shall be with all peaceableness and purity of affection."' It is the great Christian paradox that when a man discerns in himself most sin and humbles himself most, then he is really rising in the kingdom of God. (*PPS* VI, 22, pp. 320ff.)

Purity and Celibacy

Another characteristic virtue of the Christian who patterns himself on Christ is purity. A certain amount of sexual indulgence even among professed Christians was taken for granted in Newman's day. It was excused on the basis of its being part of our nature. 'We hear much in this day of the impossibility of heavenly purity,' but when men talk like this and disbelieve in the existence of severe self-rule are they sure that the impossibility does not lie in nature, but in the will? Granted that by nature we cannot will to be otherwise, but by grace we can. The question then is rather whether men have the desire for it. If they pray for it, it will be granted. By nature our wills may be in bondage, but by God's grace we will be set free. 'We obtain again, to a certain extent, the gift of free will.' (*PPS* V, 24, pp. 349–53; *Mix.*, 8, pp. 149ff.)

Newman recognized what has been the view of Christians for centuries, that temptations against purity are not overcome by direct acts of the will, but by turning the mind away from them, engaging in actions that distract the mind from them. Another method is to turn one's thoughts to Christ, recalling how He resisted temptations. Thus holy men have resisted temptations 'after our Lord's pattern and in His strength . . . not consenting to them, even in momentary acts of the will, but simply hating them, and receiving no harm from them.' In this way Christ's temptations speak comfort and encouragement to us. (*PPS* I, 3, p. 3; VI, 1, pp. 8–9)

Celibacy is in no sense a disparagement of marriage. Nor is it obligatory on the Christian. He who embraces it does so in imitation of Christ Himself, in order to be united more closely to Him. It is not to adopt a single life for its own sake. 'This is not the Virginity of the Gospel—it is not a state of independence or isolation, or dreary pride, or barren indolence or crushed affections; man is made for sympathy, for the interchange of love, for self-denial for the sake of another dearer to him than himself. The Virginity of the Christian soul is a marriage with Christ.' (*NO*, p. 277)

Ventures for Christ

Perhaps the most challenging sermon Newman preached as an Anglican was 'Ventures of Faith.' In it he asked the pointed question, 'Let every one who hears me ask himself the question, what stake has *he* in the truth of Christ's promise? . . . I really fear that most men called Christians, whatever they may profess . . . would go on almost as they do, neither much better nor much worse, if they believed Christianity to be a fable. . . . they are quiet and orderly, because it is their interest and taste to be so; but they *venture* nothing, they risk, they sacrifice, they abandon nothing on the faith of Christ's word.'

Newman cites various instances of ventures for Christ, for example, St Barnabas who gave up property in Cyprus for the poor of Christ, those who give up the promise of wealth or of eminence to become clergymen, the one who denies himself innocent pleasures as a penance for his sins, the one who prays that he may never be rich. Moreover, 'generous hearts, like James and John, or Peter, often speak . . . confidently beforehand of what they will do for Christ, not insincerely, but ignorantly. . . . "They say unto Him, We are able" . . . and in truth they were enabled to do and suffer as they had said.' And so Newman asks the challenging question, 'How is it that we are so contented with things as they are . . . that we make such excuses, if any one presses on us the necessity of something higher, the duty of bearing the Cross, if we would earn the Crown, of the Lord Jesus Christ?'

> I repeat it; what are our ventures and risks upon the truth of His word? for He says expressly, 'Every one that hath forsaken houses, or brethren, or sisters, or father, or mother, or wife, or children, or lands, for My Name's sake, shall receive an hundred-fold, and shall inherit everlasting life. But many that are first shall be last; and the last shall be first.' (*PPS* IV, sermon 20)

Chapter Twelve

Old Testament Saints and Sinners

CHRIST, though the chief pattern of holiness, is not the only one presented in Scripture for our imitation, encouragement, and instruction. There are other holy persons who despite their faults and weaknesses, their lapses into sin, served God with fidelity and perseverance. Because they were not completely perfect and without sin as Christ was, we as sinners ourselves can feel a certain human solidarity with them. In the Bible also are portrayed sinners who displeased God, incurred His wrath and punishment, and thereby serve as object lessons to teach us what actions to avoid and what motives impede our service of God.

As a boy Newman took delight in reading the Bible. After his first conversion he set himself to read it every day and as time went on he committed many parts and even whole books to memory. As a result, his acquaintance with the whole of the Bible was quite extensive. All his sermons were composed around some Scripture text, and some are simply a tissue of texts woven together into a whole. In his early preaching at St Clement's he was particularly interested not only in what he called the practical details of Christian life as recommended by the parables, for instance, but also in certain theological themes as well, such as 'the knowledge of the Gospel in the anti-deluvian World.' When he became Vicar of St Mary's, he turned his attention to Jewish History and to various Old Testament figures. He gave four different courses on Jewish history from Abraham to the Prophets, totalling twenty-five sermons in all. Some of these were later published, others have no extant manuscript, while others exist in manuscript totally or in fragments.

In the course of these sermons Newman made clear his intention. It was not to save his listeners the trouble of reading the Bible, but to lead them 'to study scriptural history and to study it rightly,—i.e. with right views of its objects and in a right Spirit.' He especially wanted to show

God's providence through the entire history of the Israelites. The scheme of salvation intended by God was time and again thwarted by men's sins and disobedience, starting in the Garden of Eden. The failure of the Israelites when they took possession of the promised land to exterminate their enemies as commanded by God, their rebellious desire for an earthly king, their falling again and again into idolatry—all these sins could not prevent God from achieving his purpose which was ultimately attained through Christ. Even when the Church was set up, men tried to divert it from its true course, as foretold by St Paul. But God works 'wisely, carrying on His plan in spite of whatever man can do.' Especially in the history of the Kings from Saul on, it is possible to trace 'God's incomprehensible foreknowledge—His deep wisdom—His silent providence gradually but surely fulfilling His decrees—His abundant mercy, patience and long-suffering—and His faithfulness, the sure ground of our hopes as Christians.' (MS sermon no. 243)

Christians cannot afford to ignore the Old Testament though its prophecies have been fulfilled in Christ. It contains permanent instructions for Christians, and is, in the words of St Paul, 'profitable for doctrine, reproof, correction, and instructions in righteousness.' (2 Tim. 3:16; MS sermon no. 236) It teaches 'deep moral lessons, such as are not vouchsafed in the New.' (*PPS* IV, 2, pp 18–19) Since much of the history in the Old Testament is merely the lives of those men who were God's instruments in their respective ages, despite the fact that some of them are not patterns for us to follow, 'yet the chief of them are specimens of especial faith and sanctity, and are set before us with the evident intention of exiting and guiding us in our religious course.' (*PPS* II, 32, p. 399) Moreover, many of these figures are types of Christ, such as Moses and David, to take but two obvious examples.

A few samples taken from different periods of Jewish history will suffice to illustrate the type of moral portrait Newman painted of various Old Testament figures, beginning with Abraham.

Abraham

Abraham's history really begins with the call from God, 'Get thee out of thy country, and from thy kindred, and from thy father's house, unto a land that I will shew thee—and I will make of thee a great nation.' (Gen. 12:1–2) This, Newman asserts, was a remarkable event in Scriptural history, 'because it is the first step in that marvelous course of divine Providence which all along had reference to Christ's coming and at length ended with it.' Turning to a consideration of Abraham's character, Newman remarks that Abraham is rightly celebrated for his faith which was remarkable given the fact that he was a faithful worshiper of the true God amidst nations that were more or less idolaters. Second, it was so strong that he broke all human connections with country and family, not knowing to what he was called. His faith was superior to ours because not all are called to give up everything for Christ, and 'our faith rests on intelligible and certain promises—we know in whom we have believed, we know the reward, eternal life.' Abraham's faith was disproportionate to his knowledge. 'No particular blessing was assigned *him* personally.' He became a wanderer all his life, 'confessing he was a stranger and pilgrim upon the earth.' Why did he do so? 'Simply *because God told him* so to do!' He preferred God to all things and acted on this. When God for example told him to send away his son Ishmael, he thought it was 'very grievous in his sight' (Gen. 20), yet at God's word he did so. This self-denying and unhesitating obedience was an act of strong faith and even more eminently so was his willingness to sacrifice his son Isaac.

Abraham was also remarkable for his humility. Trust in God implies distrust of self. Abraham spoke of himself before the Lord, 'who am I but dust and ashes.' His 'highminded generosity and disregard of his own personal advantage' were frequently displayed, as Newman showed in another sermon 'Abraham and Lot' (*PPS* III, sermon 1). Newman concluded his survey of Abraham's history by applying it to his listeners, recommending the necessity of resisting the allurements of the world to accomplish God's will and thereby to attain eternal life. They must learn to place religion first in their lives. If they do not, but make religion only a part of their daily life and not the chief object of their thoughts and actions, they must be converted, and being converted, they will then be able to engage in their worldly calling *as before but* now for the Lord's sake. Thus one's motives will be higher, and one's life 'more consistently holy, conscience more enlightened, and there will be a pleasure in self-denial, avoidance of sin, and regulation of the passions.' (MS sermon no. 202)

Moses

The history of Moses and his dealings with the Israelites reveal that he was conspicuous for his spirit of meekness, a virtue necessary for one who had to intercede for his people. Newman reminds his listeners that '*Moses was not naturally of a meek temper*—There is reason to believe he was naturally proud, passionate, impetuous,' as for example, his slaying the Egyptian he saw mistreating an Israelite. His meekness was a result of a change of character. 'It was formed in him by much struggle and self-restraint, by employing religiously the trials God put upon him, praying much and watching much, till he became gentle, patient and humble.' This is evident from a comparison of his conduct before and after he left Egypt. Despite the change, occasionally sparks of his old temper would blaze up. On one occasion, he says in God's presence, 'Wherefore hast Thou afflicted Thy servant? and wherefore have I not found favor in Thy sight, that Thou layest the burden of all this people upon me? have I conceived this people? Have I begotten them, that Thou shouldest say unto me Carry them in thy bosom . . . unto the land, which Thou swearest unto their fathers? . . . I am not able to bear all this people alone because it is too heavy for me—And if Thou deal thus with me, kill me, I pray Thee, out of hand, if I have found favor in Thy sight—and let me not see my wretchedness.' (Num. 11) The application to Christians was easy and obvious: a Christian can change and does so with God's grace. (MS sermon no. 210)

'The history of Moses is valuable to Christians,' Newman asserted, 'not only as giving us a pattern of fidelity towards God, of great firmness, and great meekness, but also as affording a type or figure of our Saviour Christ.' Newman develops the similarity between Moses and Christ. We are born in a spiritual Egypt, slaves to the Devil. Like Pharaoh he is a hard task-master. Such is our state by nature. As Moses rescued the Israelites from Egypt so Christ has broken the power of the Devil. 'He leads us forth on our way, and makes a path through all difficulties, that we may go forward towards heaven.' As Moses told the Israelites at the Red Sea, 'Stand still, and see the salvation of God,' so Christ has spoken to us. By trusting in Christ we are enabled to do things above our strength; we overcome our sins, surrender our wishes, conquer ourselves, making a way through the powers of the world, the flesh, and the devil. Christ leads us from hell to heaven.

Second, Christ reveals to us the will of God, as Moses did to the Israelites. He is our Prophet, as well as our Redeemer. 'Before Christ came, Moses alone saw God face to face; all prophets after him but heard His voice or saw Him in vision.' Yet Moses was allowed only to see 'the skirts of God's greatness.' 'But Christ really saw, and ever saw the face of God, . . . for he was the Only-begotten Son.' 'In Him God is fully and truly seen, so that He is absolutely the Way, and the Truth and the Life.' Hence, He brings us knowledge, wisdom, and above all grace whereby we may be 'changed into the same image from glory to glory.'

Third, Moses was the great intercessor when the Israelites sinned. So is Christ, but Moses could not make up for a single sin. Moses was not taken instead of Israel, except in figure, and Moses suffered for his own sin and was not allowed to enter the promised land, but 'Christ was the spotless Lamb of God,' who suffered not for His own sins but ours, and His death really gained our pardon; it was meritorious. (*PPS* VII, sermon 9)

Saul

Newman introduced his narratives of the Kings of Israel with a sermon that served as a prelude, 'Wilfulness of Israel in Rejecting Samuel.' (*PPS* III, sermon 2) When the Israelites entered the promised land, they were commanded by God to exterminate their enemies and not to intermarry with the peoples they found there. These commands they failed to obey and God allowed them to be sorely harassed by their enemies as a punishment. Despite His many mercies to them, when they called upon Him for help, they fell again and again into idolatry. Moreover, the Israelites were told from the beginning not to act on their own initiative, but to wait for God's guidance and to follow it. '"*Be still,* and know that I am God." Move not, speak not—look to the pillar of the cloud, see how *it* moves—then follow.'

Once again the Israelites defied this command when they demanded a king like the nations around them, in order, as they put it, 'to judge us, and go out before us, and fight our battles.' But this was exactly what

God had done for them under Samuel. 'There was an additional aggravation of their sin; they had really been promised a king, at some future time undetermined, by Moses himself. . . . The fact that God had promised what they clamoured for, and merely claimed to choose the time, surely ought to have satisfied them. But they were headstrong; and He answered them according to their wilfulness. He "gave them a king in His anger."' This king was Saul. In his sermon by that name, Newman traced the history of Saul and allowed the concluding judgment to emerge naturally from the narrative, namely, 'unbelief and wilfulness are the wretched characteristics of Saul's history—an ear deaf to the plainest commands, a heart hardened against the most gracious influences.' (*PPS* III, sermon 3)

The history of Saul and his moral character continued to fascinate Newman, partly because of his mysteriousness, as mentioned first in 'Saul' and then again in a later sermon, 'Wilfulness the Sin of Saul.' Commenting on the mysteriousness of God's selecting an instrument of His purpose whom He foresaw would not fulfill it, Newman remarks that though Saul was given in anger, 'this does not show that a man was chosen who was *sure not* to do God's will; merely that God left things to themselves and, after choosing an instrument (humanly speaking) likely to fulfil it, yet suffered the wickedness and unbelief of His whole people to be exemplified *in the instance* of their King—He was a specimen of the whole self-willed race.' (MS sermon no. 243)

For Saul was eminently qualified to maintain political power at home and to strike terror into the surrounding nations. Leaders are generally not of a mild, pliant, and amiable nature, but made of sterner stuff. So it was with Saul. Pride and sullenness, obstinacy and impetuosity characterized Saul, yet such qualities, when opened to the power of the Holy Spirit, 'become transformed into zeal, firmness, and high-mindedness of religious Faith. It depended on Saul himself whether or not he became the rival of that exalted saint, who, being once a fierce avenger of his brethren, at length became "the meekest of men," yet not losing thereby, but gaining, moral strength and resolution.' (*US,* 9, pp. 166–67) Why he did not become a St Paul was because he failed the test provided by God. It is the dramatic presentation of this test that makes the 'Trial of Saul' perhaps the most powerful of all Newman's sermons on Old Testament figures.

What was Saul's trial? The Israelites, over whom Saul was appointed to reign, had been oppressed and harassed by their enemies, particularly the Philistines who far outnumbered the Israelites when they drew up opposite them at Gilgal. Before Saul went to battle, it was necessary to offer a burnt sacrifice to the Lord, and to beg of Him a blessing on the arms of Israel. Only priest and prophets, however, could do this. Saul had to wait seven days for Samuel to come, 'but Samuel came not to Gilgal, and the people were scattered from him.' Newman dramatizes this situation in which Saul, though seeing his army crumbling away, his soldiers afraid and deserting him, and the enemy ready to attack, nevertheless obeys God and the prophet. He looks out for Samuel's coming.

But when his trial seemed over, a second one awaited him, for the prophet of God does not come as he said he would. Hitherto Saul had had faith and trust in God; he should have continued to trust. 'God fights not with sword and bow; He can give victory to whom He will, and when He will; "with His own right hand, and His holy arm," can He accomplish His purposes.' Saul had proof because the enemy had not attacked, but he did not feel this, and so he took a rash and fatal step; he offered the burnt offering himself, and no sooner had he done it, a crime denounced in Scripture, than Samuel came. And so he failed the test. Had he waited one more hour Samuel would have come. The consequence was that he lost God's favor, and forfeited his kingdom.

When Samuel asks him what he had done, Saul offers his excuse, but Samuel replies, 'Thou hast done foolishly: thou hast not kept the commandment of the Lord thy God, which He commanded thee: for now would the Lord have established thy kingdom upon Israel for ever. But now thy kingdom shall not continue: the Lord hath sought Him a man after His own heart, and the Lord hath commanded him to be captain over His people, because thou hast not kept that which the Lord commanded thee.'

Newman then develops an analogy between Saul and the Christian. As Saul, being anointed with oil by Samuel, became King of Israel, so we by baptism are kings, not of this world but kings and princes in the heavenly kingdom of Christ. Though poor in this world, yet when we are baptized, 'we, like Saul, were made strong in the Lord, powerful princes, with Angels to wait upon us, and with a place on Christ's throne in prospect.' Favored by God like Saul, like Saul we are put on trial, and how many fall like him. How many tell lies or steal to get out of a difficult situation, offering excuses, or like Saul not casting off religion entirely but wanting to choose their own way of being religious. Others like Saul bear a trial for a time but fall. Newman warns 'Let us watch and pray. Let us not get secure,' and concludes, 'God give us grace to be in the number of those . . . who sincerely wish to know God's will, and who do it as far as they know it.' (*PPS* VIII, sermon 3)[1]

David

God's will could not be thwarted by the disobedience of Saul and the people. God wanted a king after His own heart, and one is found in David, whom Newman eulogizes in his sermon, 'The Early Years of David.' (*PPS* III, sermon 4) In many respects David is the most favored of all the ancient saints, 'the principal type of Christ,' the author of a great part of the book of Psalms, 'a chief instrument of God's providence, both in repressing idolatry and in preparing for the gospel, and he prophesied in an especial manner of that Saviour whom he prefigured and preceded.' Pride disgraced the history of the chosen people, but David was 'conspicuous for an affectionate, a thankful, a loyal heart towards his God and defender, a zeal which was as fervent and as docile as Saul's was sullen, and as keensighted and as pure as Balaam's was selfish and double-minded.'

Newman then traces the history of David's early years, when after being anointed by Samuel he was tried by God and showed himself humble, notwithstanding the temptation 'of acting without God's guidance, when he had the means of doing so.' Jeroboam afterwards failed the test. Several times after Saul's attempts on his life, David held Saul's life in his hands, but he kept his reverence for God's anointed: 'The Lord forbid that I should do this thing unto my master, the Lord's anointed, to stretch forth mine hand against him, seeing he is the anointed of the Lord.' What then was the special grace or distinguishing virtue of David as faith was Abraham's, meekness that of Moses, self-mastery the special trait of Joseph? David's 'peculiar excellence' is '*fidelity to the trust committed to him*; a firm, uncompromising singlehearted devotion to the cause of God, and a burning zeal for His honour.' Those traits as manifested in

David's rescuing the ark of the covenant, and in preparing the material for the building of the temple, Newman develops in a subsequent sermon (MS sermon no. 242). Yet David was not allowed to build the temple; this was reserved for his son Solomon.

Comparing David with other figures of the Old Testament, Newman says, 'He inherits the prompt faith and magnanimity of Abraham; he is simple as Isaac; he is humble as Jacob; he has the youthful wisdom and self-possession, the tenderness, the affectionateness, and the firmness of Joseph. And, as his own especial gift, he has an overflowing thankfulness, an ever-burning devotion, a zealous fidelity to his God, a high unshaken loyalty towards his king, an heroic bearing in all circumstances, such as the multitude of men see to be great, but cannot understand.' Newman then makes a point as he frequently does with regards to the saints: 'Contrast one with another the Scripture Saints; how different are they, yet how alike! how fitted for their respective circumstances, yet how unearthly, how settled and composed in the faith and fear of God.'

Jeremiah

Of the Old Testament figures one whom Newman admired and brought to mind at various times during his life was Jeremiah. Newman introduces the narrative of Jeremiah's life with some summary remarks on the prophets in general, namely, that the earlier prophets though hated and thwarted by the wicked were held in honor and exalted to high places in the congregation of the people. Such were Moses, Samuel, and David. The later prophets were not only feared and hated by the enemies of God, but cast out of the vineyard. In their sufferings they preshadowed the Great Prophet whose way they were preparing: in their suffering, the priesthood of Christ, in their teaching, His prophetical office, and in their miracles, the royal power. The history of Jeremiah, which is narrated most fully in Scripture, 'is the most exact type of Christ' next to David. Newman considers Jeremiah a specimen of all those prophets spoken of in the Epistle to the Hebrews as an example of faith, and by St James as an example of patience.

The reformation of Josiah which had taken place in the early years of Jeremiah would certainly have impressed Jeremiah, and so, Newman says, one can presume he began his labors with encouragement and hope. Soon, however, his hopes were destroyed and 'his mind sobered, into a more blessed and noble temper,—resignation.' 'To expect great effects from our exertions for religious objects is natural indeed . . . but it arises from inexperience of the kind of work we have to do,—to change the heart and will of man. It is a far nobler frame of mind, to labour, not with the hope of seeing the fruit of our labour, but for conscience' sake, as a matter of duty; and again, in faith, trusting good *will* be done, though we see it not.' Newman then cites as instances of God's servants beginning with success, but ending with disappointment Moses, Samuel, Elijah, Isaiah, and also the apostles of Christ.

All the various emotions and feelings Jeremiah experienced in his transition from hope to disappointment and resignation are expressed and recorded in Scripture. He is tortured, put into prison, falsely accused, sent into exile. He undergoes affliction, fear, despondency, restlessness until they ended in resignation.

Newman applied this to himself and his listeners. Though our trials differ, still 'that disappointment in some shape or other is the lot of man . . . is plain from the mere fact . . . that we begin life with health and end it with sickness, or in other words, that it *comes* to an *end,* for an end is a failure.' Experience of life suggests this conclusion, what of religion? Scripture teaches us to expect disappointment and suffering, but to accept it humbly when God sends it, as behooves a sinner. We must persevere in faith and trust, taking up the cross of Christ. We mourn in order to rejoice more perfectly.

> Begin on faith; you cannot see at first whither He is leading you, and how light will arise out of darkness. You must begin by denying yourselves your natural wishes,—a painful work; by refraining from sin, by rousing from sloth, by preserving your tongue from insincere words, and your hands from deceitful dealings, and your eyes from beholding vanity; by watching against the first rising of anger, pride, impurity, obstinacy, jealousy; by learning to endure the laugh of irreligious men for Christ's sake; by forcing your minds to follow seriously the words of prayer, though it be difficult to you, and by keeping before you the thought of God all through the day. These things you will be able to do if you do but seek the mighty help of God the Holy Spirit which is given you. . . . 'And the Lord shall guide you continually, and satisfy your

soul in drought: and you shall be like a watered garden, and like a spring of water, whose waters fail not.' (*PPS* VIII, sermon 9)[2]

Conclusion

In Jeremiah Newman constantly found consolation and encouragement. Indeed, he found the same in meditating upon all the figures in Scripture who lived and died in faith. In Scripture 'we find that we are not solitary; that others, before us, have been in our very condition, have had our feelings, undergone our trials, and laboured for the price which we are seeking.' They are our brethren. One 'finds, in the history of the past, a peculiar kind of consolation counteracting the influence of the world that is seen. What a world of sympathy and comfort is thus opened to us in the Communion of Saints! . . . Are we young, and in temptation or trial? we cannot be in worse circumstances than Joseph. Are we in sickness? Job will surpass us in sufferings as in patience. Are we in perplexities and anxieties, with conflicting duties and a bewildered mind, having to please unkind superiors, yet without offending God; so grievous a trial as David's we cannot have, when Saul persecuted him. Is it our duty to witness for the truth among sinners? No Christian can at this day be so hardly circumstanced as Jeremiah. Have we domestic trials? Job, Jacob, and David were afflicted in their children. . . . a man, who has never thought of the history of the Saints, will gain little benefit from it on first taking up the subject when he comes into trouble. . . . The consolation in question comes not in the way of argument but by habit.' (*PPS* III, 17, pp. 243–46; see also *PPS* III, 4, pp. 58–59) Newman's sermons testify that he had indeed acquired the habit.

Notes

1. This is not the only instance in Old Testament history that Newman points out God's punishing someone for assuming the role of priest. See the sermon, 'The Gainsaying of Korah,' *PPS* IV, sermon 18.

2. Newman preached this sermon 12 September 1830 just after the failure of his efforts to reform the Church Missionary and Bible Societies and to make the Oriel tutorship more a pastoral than a mere secular office. He said it was in his mind all during the Oxford Movement. (*LD* II, 289, n. 1; XXIV, 272–73)

Chapter Thirteen

Christian Saints

Honoring the Saints

The Church on earth is surrounded by an invisible 'cloud of witnesses' whose lives, especially those recorded both in the Old and the New Testaments, are an inspiration and encouragement to us. We are not alone, but part of this throng. In March 1830 Newman introduced Saints' Days services in St Mary's. In a sermon preached on All Saints' Day, 30 November 1831, speaking of the honor paid to the saints he remarked that 'not even the world itself could contain the records of His love, the history of those many Saints, that "cloud of witnesses," whom we to-day celebrate.' These are 'Martyrs and Confessors, Rulers and Doctors of the Church, devoted Ministers and Religious brethren, kings of the earth and all people, princes and judges of the earth, young men and maidens, old men and children, the first fruits of all ranks, ages, and callings, gathered each in his own time into the paradise of God.' The special benefit to be derived from the observance of Saints' Days 'lies in their setting before the mind the patterns of excellence for us to follow.' In so doing the Church follows the example of Scripture which portrays for us the lives of those men who were God's special instruments, the chief of them, specimens of 'faith and sanctity,' to guide us in our spiritual course. (*PPS* II, 32, pp. 393–94, 399)

As a Catholic Newman reiterated this view. The Saints 'are always our standard of right and good; they are raised up to be monuments and lessons, they remind us of God, they introduce us into the unseen world, they teach us what Christ loves, they track out for us the way which leads heavenward. They are to us who see them . . . objects of our veneration and of our homage.' (*Mix.*, p. 102)

Martyrs

The first saints were martyrs. The word properly means, says Newman, 'a *witness* but is used to denote exclusively one who has suffered *death* for the Christian faith. Those who have witnessed for Christ without suffering death, are called *Confessors;* a title which the early Martyrs often made their own, before their last solemn confession unto death, or Martyrdom.' (*PPS* II, 4, p. 41) Speaking of the early martyrs in the Church he makes some interesting and unusual points. To be a martyr in the early Church was 'to be a *voluntary* sufferer.' They knew in advance the consequence of their preaching the gospel; Christ had foretold it. They were subjected to threats and inducements to desert Christ. 'Death, their final suffering, was but the consummation of a life of anticipated death.' They were *harassed,* 'shaken as wheat in a sieve,' in accordance with the statement of Christ, 'Satan hath desired to have you, that he may sift you as wheat.' Under such circumstances even the bold-hearted are tempted to give up because of the incessant harassment. Thus, the Church was sifted, the cowardly falling off, the faithful continuing firm, though in dejection and perplexity.

The death of these martyrs had a special quality about it. 'It was a death, cruel in itself, publicly inflicted: and heightened by the fierce exultation of a malevolent populace. . . . The unseen God alone was their Comforter, and this invests the scene of their suffering with supernatural majesty.' It involved a fellowship with Christ's suffering, 'a kind of sacrament, a baptism of blood.' Newman does not draw the usual lesson of asking for grace to withstand enemies of our faith even unto the shedding of our blood, or the lesson of faith, but rather of humility. 'By contemplating the lowest of His true servants, and seeing how far any one of them surpasses ourselves, we learn to shrink before His ineffable purity, who is infinitely holier than the holiest of His creatures; and to confess ourselves with a sincere mind to be unworthy of the least of all His mercies. Thus His Martyrs lead us to Himself, the chief of Martyrs and the King of Saints.' (*PPS* II, 4, p. 49)

The Influence of the Saints

As he explained in the *Apologia,* Newman based his efforts on behalf of the Oxford Movement on the principle of personality. In a sermon preached almost two years prior to the beginning of the Movement he attempted to show that Truth was upheld, 'not as a system, not by books, not by argument, nor by temporal power, but by the personal influence of such men . . . who are at once the teachers and the patterns of it.' Of the qualities that make for such influence one of the first is holiness. 'The attraction, exerted by unconscious holiness, is of an urgent and irresistible nature.' Moreover, if it exerts an influence over the 'thoughtless and perverse multitude,' what must be its power 'over that select number . . . who have already, in a measure, disciplined their hearts after the law of holiness.' Such teachers of Truth as the latter are hidden and few, but 'they are enough to carry on God's noiseless work. The Apostles were such men; others might be named, in their several generations, as successors to their holiness. . . . A few highly-endowed men will rescue the world for centuries.' Newman cites the example of St Athanasius who impressed his image on the Church for ages to come. 'Such men . . . light their beacons on the heights. Each receives and transmits the sacred flame, trimming it in rivalry of his predecessor.' (*US*, 5, pp. 91–96)

Consequently, those who make the most noise or seem to be principals in the change and events recorded in history, are not necessarily the most useful men nor the most favored by God. If we would trace truly 'the hand of God in human affairs . . . we must . . . turn our eyes to private life, watching in all we read or witness for the true signs of God's presence, the graces of personal holiness in His elect; which, weak as they may seem to mankind, are mighty through God, and have an influence upon the course of His Providence, and bring about great events in the world at large, when the wisdom and strength of the natural man are of no avail.' They are truly 'the world's benefactors.' (*PPS* II, 1, pp. 4–5; *CS*, p. 42)

The Hidden Ones

In a poem, 'The Hidden Ones' Newman wrote of the obscurity yet radiance of the saints.

> Hid are the saints of God;—
> Uncertified by high angelic sign;

> Christ rears His throne within the secret heart,
>   From the haughty world apart.
>
>   Yet not all-hid from those
> Who watch to see;—'neath their dull guise of earth,
> Bright bursting gleams unwittingly disclose
>   Their heaven-wrought birth.
> Meekness, love, patience, faith's serene repose. (*VV*, pp. 42–43)

The saints though hidden exercise enormous power. 'A really holy man, a true saint, though he looks like other men, still has a sort of secret power in him to attract others to him who are like-minded, and to influence all who have anything in them like him.' So much is this so that it is often a test whether we have the mind of the saints, whether they have influence over us. (*PPS* IV, 16, p. 244) The holier a man is, the less he is understood by men of the world. The title of saint is not given them until after death, when their excellence becomes more widely known. They then become examples and pledges 'of all those other high creations of God, His saints in full number, who die and are never known.' (*PPS* IV, 10, p. 157)

If it is asked why God's saints are not known immediately, there are other reasons beyond the fact that their good deeds were done in secret. Good men are often slandered and ill-treated in their lifetime; they offend by their holiness; their intentions and aims misunderstood, some of their good deeds are known to some men, not to all. Only after death when envy and anger have died away, can they be vindicated and a more exact estimate be made of all their works and deeds. (*PPS* IV, 10, pp. 157–58)

How does the saint of God whom the Church honors differ from the ordinary Christian? He does so in this, 'that he sets before him as the one object of life, to please and obey God; that he ever aims to submit his will to God's will; that he earnestly follows after holiness; and that he is habitually striving to have a closer resemblance to Christ in all things.' The ordinary Christian, however, never makes such an effort. He thinks it fair to resent insults and repay wrongs, to insist on his rights, to seek to be rich, to do well in the world, to fear what his neighbors will say. He rarely thinks of Judgment, says few prayers, cares little for the Church, and spends his money on himself. (*PPS* IV, 10, pp. 157–59)

It should be recalled, however, by way of comfort and encouragement, that 'there has not been one who was not hewn out of the same rock as the most obdurate of reprobates . . . not one who was not by nature brother of those poor souls who . . . are lost in hell. Grace has vanquished nature; that is the whole history of the Saints . . . wonderful news for those who sorrowfully recognize in their hearts the vast difference that exists between them and the Saints; joyful news, when men hate sin, and wish to escape from its miserable yoke, yet are tempted to think it impossible!' (*Mix.,* pp. 48–49)

Variety of Saints

In one way all the saints are alike, resembling each other in this, 'that their excellence is supernatural, their deeds heroic, their merits extraordinary and prevailing. They all are choice patterns of the theological virtues; they all are blessed with a rare and special union with their Maker and Lord; they all lead lives of penance, and when they leave this world, they are spared that torment, which the multitude of holy souls are allotted, between earth and heaven, death and eternal glory.' (*OS,* 7, p. 91)

Nevertheless, there are different types of saints. Some have lived without deliberate sin from childhood; others only after a sinful youth have been brought by God's grace to repentance. Others have been called 'not from vice and ungodliness, but from a life of mere ordinary blamelessness, or from a state of lukewarmness, or from thoughtlessness, to heroical greatness, and these have often given up lands, and property, and honours, and station, and repute, for Christ's sake.' In the early days of the Church many martyrs bore cruel and prolonged tortures rather than deny their faith in Christ. Others have been extraordinary missionaries in foreign lands; others devoted themselves to the redemption of Christian slaves from pagan or Mahometan masters; others to taking care of the sick in time of pestilences; others to the instruction of the poor; others to the education of children; others to preaching and confessional work; others to study and to prayer; others to a life of intercession and prayer. (*Mix.,* pp. 100–101)

Saints also differ from one another in that the qualities they have in common are differently combined in each of them: 'one Saint is remarkable for fortitude; not that he has not other heroic virtues by *concomitance*, as it may be called, but by virtue of that one gift in particular he has won his crown.' It gives form to all the rest grouped around it. 'Thus it is that often what is right in one would be wrong in another; and in fact, the very same action is allowed or chosen by one, and shunned by another, as being consistent or inconsistent with their respective characters,—pretty much as in the combination of colours, each separate tint takes a shade from the rest, and is good or bad from its company. The whole gives a meaning to the parts.' Hence, the saints are not to be imitated in a slavish way; their practices are not always to be followed. (*HS* II, pp. 228–29; *PPS* VI, 3, pp. 34–35)

Even so the variety of the saints reveals God's workmanship, 'but whatever was their special line of duty, they have been heroes in it; they have attained such noble self-command . . . they have sustained such great and continued pains, they have persevered in such vast labours . . . that they have been the means of setting up a standard before us of truth, of magnanimity, of holiness, of love.' (*Mix.*, p. 101)

The Fathers of the Church

As a boy Newman became enamored of the Fathers of the Church from the long extracts he read of St Augustine, St Ambrose, and the other Fathers in Milner's *Church History*. This love increased when he read them in depth. At the beginning of the Oxford Movement he began to read through Tillemont's sixteen-volume work, *Mémoires pour servir à l'histoire ecclésiastique des six premiers siècles* to find material for his sketches, 'The Church of the Fathers,' which were printed in the *British Magazine*. To the then urgent question, what to do if the State casts off the Church, Newman found an answer in the life of St Ambrose, who was able to appeal to the people in his contests with the civil authorities, and thus the Church found favor with the people without any subservience to them. As he continued the series Newman used these sketches to promote Catholic principles, such as celibacy, fasting, asceticism, and monasticism, which were anathema to the Protestant mentality in the Church.

Although these writings were in one way polemical, they were mainly historical. At the same time Newman strove to get at the personality of
the saint he was dealing with. Nor did he overlook their faults. As an
example Newman writes of St Gregory,

> We have a picture of a man of warm affections, amiable disposition, and
> innocent life. As a son, full of piety, tenderness, and watchful solicitude;
> as a friend or companion, lively, cheerful, and open-hearted; overflowing
> with natural feelings, and easy in his expression of them; simple, good,
> humble, primitive. His aspirations were high, as became a saint, his life
> ascetic in the extreme, and his conscience still more sensitive of sin and
> infirmity. At the same time, he was subject to alternations of feeling;
> was deficient all along in strength of mind and self-control; and was
> harassed, even in his old age, by irritability, fear, and other passions,
> which one might think that even years, not to say self-discipline, would
> have brought into subjection. Such mere temptations and infirmities in
> no way interfere with his being a Saint, and, since they do not, it is
> consolatory to our weak hearts and feeble wills to find from the precedent
> of Gregory, that, being what we are, we nevertheless may be in God's
> favour. (*HS* II, pp. 80–81)

The Lives of the English Saints

It is not necessary to enter into a detailed account of Newman's intentions
with regard to the project he proposed of a series of lives of the English
saints in 1843. Certain points, however, need to be made. Newman had
hoped that the series would combine devotion and history, but in using
the available hagiographic sources the problem was how to satisfy the
claims of historical criticism with the handling of legends which were
mixed with the accounts, or put another way, how can one deal with all
that has been said and believed of saints, when there is so little historical
foundation for it. There is no way of separating the facts inextricably
linked with the fiction. Legends were used by the hagiographer to bring
out the action of some principle, point of character, and the like, and this
is its religious purpose. The only thing to do then was to accept what has
survived and been handed down as symbolical of the unknown, and use it
for a religious purpose in a religious way. What is important, however, is

that Newman was conscious of the distinction between history and devotion, and between the historian and the hagiographer.[1] This distinction he continued to maintain.

Introduction to a Proposed Life of St Philip Neri

In 1853 Newman composed what turned out to be but a fragment of a life of St Philip Neri. In the introduction he elaborates in greater detail the distinction between history and devotion. There are two types of saints' lives, he wrote. On the one hand there is the piecemeal life of a saint such as is gained from a canonical process for canonization, which separated the saint into his virtues. Each portion has its own instruction aside from the whole. Newman himself had the previous year made such a selection from the life of St Philip Neri for refectory reading and called it 'lessons out of St Philip's Life for every day of the year.' The limitation of such lives is that it makes little difference from the point of view of religious instruction whether or not the virtue was practiced by this particular saint. Newman referred to this as a *devotional* life, as distinct from a *historical* one.

On the other hand, there is another method whereby the saints are presented 'as living and breathing men, as persons and invested with personal attributes and a character of their own, and peculiarities of habit and feeling and opinion such as belong to him and not to another.' This method he compares to St Ignatius' method in the *Spiritual Exercises* of bringing the scene and the persons before the imagination.' In such lives the saints are not merely objects of spiritual reading which are limited to spiritual subjects. A saint's life also contains things not directly or immediately spiritual but simply human. 'To find a Saint sitting down to cards, or reading a heathen author, or listening to music, or taking snuff, is often a relief and encouragement to the reader.' How different this is 'from the shadowy paper-Saint,' which unconnected details convey and what may make the reader shrink from the Saints and discourage him.' (*NO,* pp. 257–59)

This was the type of life Newman wanted to write of St Philip Neri, for which he continued to collect material but which he never wrote. He wanted, he said, to convey not only his actions but the man himself, in particular he wanted to have such a living view of him that he could show how apparently irreconcilable points in his conduct could be understood and go together with each. It was this view which Newman could not get from the different documents in the canonical process; rather he found four or five different persons, unreconciled with each other.

The same criticism of saints' lives Newman made in the introduction to his 'Final Years of St John Chrysostom,' where he called this chopping up of the saint into his virtues 'a series of points of meditation on particular virtues, but not the life of a saint as a living whole.' Newman wanted a life which would impress the reader with 'the idea of a moral unity, identity, growth, continuity, personality.' Such a view of a saint cannot be obtained from a narrative of his actions alone. 'Actions are not enough for sanctity; we must have saintly motives; and as to these motives, the actions themselves seldom carry the motives along with them.' Hence, a life must deal with the interior of the saint, and this is best obtained not from the guesses or judgments of the biographer, but rather from the writings, especially the letters of the saints. The availability of such material was one of the main reasons for his preference for the ancient saints. Moreover, in popular lives of the saints Newman deprecated the suppression of facts, or glosses put upon facts, because of 'an endemic perennial fidget which possess us about giving scandal, whereas of all scandals such omissions, such glosses, are the greatest.' (*HS* II, pp. 217–31)

Individual Saints

When one examines Newman's writings on individual saints, the foregoing distinctions enable one to classify them and to understand why some are more successful than others. Moreover, most of Newman's writings about individual saints are contained in sermons whose purpose is religious, devotional, and spiritual rather than historical. The sermons on saints in Scripture in volume 2 of *Parochial and Plain Sermons* fall into Newman's category of devotion. They tell little about the saints themselves. Allowing for the fact that there is relatively little known about these saints from Scripture, still one sees that they are appropriate figures for developing a spiritual lesson or even to inculcate a dogmatic truth. For example, St Thomas is the occasion for a sermon on faith, St John for one on the love of relatives and friends, St Peter for a discussion of Christian ministers as representatives of Christ. We come away with little remembrance of the saint himself and still less of his unique personality.

Perhaps the most successful sermon in this category is 'Purity and Love,' in which St John the Baptist and St John the Evangelist are taken as representative of purity, while St Peter and St Paul, Mary Magdalen, St Augustine, and St Ignatius represent love, not that these two virtues can be completely separated from each other. The emphasis in the sermon is placed on the latter group. These the Good Shepherd led from service to Satan by extinguishing a carnal love and inspiring a heavenly charity. The presentation of the scene in which Mary Magdalen washes the feet of Christ is an Ignatian contemplation in which one is placed vividly in the scene. This enables Newman to appeal to his hearers to repent and return to God.

On the other hand, there are several sermons which leave a strong impression of the saint even if they do not fulfill completely the demands Newman himself set down for a historical life. Though they do not attempt an account of the entire life of the saint, they manage nevertheless to convey a vivid picture of the uniqueness of the individual *personality,* as distinct from that of other saints. Such are the two sermons on St Paul the Apostle and the long Discourse in two parts on Philip Neri, for both of whom Newman had a special veneration and devotion.

St Paul

In the sermon, 'St Paul's Characteristic Gift,' Newman affirms that as St Paul had human nature so strong within him, he was able to enter into human nature wherever he encountered it, and to sympathize with it, 'with a gift peculiarly his own.' The Apostle of the Gentiles ranges himself among 'the children of wrath.' He speaks of concupiscence as if it were sin 'because he vividly apprehended in that nature of his which grace had sanctified, what it was in its tendencies and results when deprived of grace.' He identifies himself with human nature wherever it is found, whether in Jew or Gentile.

St Paul's feeling for his own race was a 'special mixture, bitter and sweet, of generous pride . . . but of piercing, overwhelming anguish,' because they 'had the birthright and the promise, yet who, instead of making use of them, had madly thrown them away.' '"Who are Israelites," he says, mournfully lingering over their past glories, "who are Israelites, to whom belongeth the adoption of children, and the glory, and the testament, and the giving of the law, and the service of God, and the promises: whose are the fathers, and of whom is Christ according to the flesh, who is over all things, God blessed for ever. Amen."' He pleaded for them while they were persecuting his Lord and himself, reminding Him that he too had once been His persecutor. 'I wish myself to be anathema from Christ, for my kinsmen according to the flesh.' He takes comfort in the thought of 'his confident anticipation of their recovery in time to come.' (*OS*, sermon 7)

In another sermon, 'St Paul's Gift of Sympathy,' Newman developed more fully this gift of sympathy. He says of St Paul that he almost forgets his gifts and privileges, his dignity as an apostle and speaks as 'a frail man speaking to frail men, and he is tender towards the weak from a sense of his own weakness.' After revealing his own special revelations, he remarks, 'Lest the greatness of the revelation should exalt me, there was given me a sting of my flesh . . . to buffet me.' And praying to be rid of it, the Lord said to him, 'My grace is sufficient for thee, for power is made perfect in infirmity.' 'Gladly, therefore, will I glory in my infirmities, that the power of Christ may dwell in me,' comments St. Paul.

St Paul shares with his converts the knowledge of his own tribulations, and 'speaks to them as their equal rather than as an Apostle, and reminds them, "You know from the first day I came into Asia, in what manner I have been with you for all the time, serving the Lord with all humility, and with tears, and temptations."' Such ability to sympathize with others created the conditions both to conceive great love for others and to elicit love from them, as is borne out by the record of his farewell visit to his brethren at Ephesus, Tyre, and Caesarea before departing to suffer in Jerusalem. 'There was much weeping among them all; and, falling on the neck of Paul, they kissed him, being grieved most of all for the word that he had said, that they should see his face no more.'

His love extended not merely to his converts but to his special friends and co-laborers in the apostolate. So Newman concludes, 'St Paul loved his brethren. He lived in them; he felt with them and for them; he was anxious about them, he gave them help, and in turn looked for comfort from them. His mind was like some instrument of music, harp or viol, the strings of which vibrate, though untouched, by the noises which other instruments give forth, and he was ever, according to his own precept, "rejoicing with them that rejoice, and weeping with them that weep;" . . . "Who is weak," he asks, "and I am not weak? who is scandalized, and I am not on fire?" And, after saying this, he characteristically adds, "If I must needs glory, I will glory of the things that concern my infirmity."'

Newman concluded the sermon with a comparison of St Paul and St ,Philip Neri, who loved to read and meditate upon Paul's Epistles. Despite the differences between the two, they are alike in this, 'putting aside forms . . . and letting influence take the place of rule, and charity stand instead of authority, they drew souls to them by their interior beauty, and held them captive by the regenerate affections of human nature.' (OS, sermon 8)

St Philip Neri

'The Mission of St Philip' was a lecture given on the first anniversary of the Oratory being set up in Birmingham. Since it antedated the fragment of a life of Philip mentioned above, obviously Newman did not feel he had achieved the goal of a historical life which would show a unity between the different Philips at different stages of his life. Nor could this be achieved in the course of a two-part lecture, however lengthy. Nevertheless Newman brilliantly and succinctly captures the spirit of the Renaissance, the time in which Philip lived, and he describes Savonarola's career so that later he can contrast it with that of Philip. He traces the successive influence of St Benedict, St Dominic, and St Ignatius on Philip, and contrasts or compares St Philip with Savonarola, who began with an external reform. He burned lutes and guitars, looking glasses and masks, books and pictures, in the public square, 'but St Philip bore with every outside extravagance in those whom he addressed, as far as it was not directly sinful, knowing well that if the heart was once set right, the appropriate demeanour would follow.'

Philip could not endure harsh rebukes, anything like rigor. 'He allured men to the service of God . . . he accommodated himself to the temper of each, as, in the words of the Apostle, to become "all things to all men, that he might gain all."'' Savonarola preached; St Philip discoursed and conversed. As a result he exercised enormous influence on persons of all ranks and classes of society, who came to him for confession and instruction.

The special spirit of Philip, however, was that of the humble priest, shrinking from every kind of dignity, or post, or office. He did not want to be opposed or maligned, but simply to be overlooked, to be despised, 'to despise the whole world,' he said, 'to despise no member of it, to despise oneself, *to despise being despised.*' He took great pleasure in being undervalued, and always attempted to hide his great devotion, and he would try simply to cover any virtuous act. It was this same spirit that Newman wished his own congregation to have, to work hard, to be overlooked, to work for God alone 'with a pure heart and single eye, without the distraction of human applause,' and make Him their sole hope, and His eternal heaven their sole aim. (*OS*, sermon 12, pp. 199–242)

The Ancient Saints

Perhaps Newman came closest to his ideal of a historical life of a saint in his series of articles, 'The Ancient Saints,' dealing with the last years of St John Chrysostom. In them the details of Chrysostom's last years are presented in an interesting narrative with copious quotations from his letters. At the same time Newman tried to uncover what he thought the traits were that made Chrysostom different from other saints, not what he had in common with them, and this he affirmed, resided in 'the interest he takes in all things, not so far as God has made them alike, but as He has made them different from each other. I speak of the discriminating affectionateness with which he accepts every one for what is personal in him and unlike others. I speak of his versatile recognition of men, one by one, for the sake of that portion of good . . . which has severally been lodged in them; his eager contemplation of the many things they do, effect, or produce. . . . I speak of the kindly spirit and genial temper with which he looks round at all things which this wonderful world contains; of the graphic fidelity with which he notes them down upon the tablets of his mind, and of the promptitude and propriety with which he calls them up as arguments or illustrations in the course of his teaching as occasion requires.' It is this power of throwing himself into the minds of others that, for Newman, constituted the charm of his method of exposition of the Scriptures by expounding its literal sense. (*HS*, II, pp. 286–89)

Because of his difficulties with the *Rambler* magazine Newman did not continue the series of articles he planned on the ancient saints in succession to those on St John Chrysostom. This is unfortunate since from the evidence of the work on the latter, he was well on his way to achieving the ideal of a life of a saint, one that combined a history of the life, with analysis of motives, and a distinct spiritual portrait based upon the details of the saint's life and activities.

It is this type of life which the Congregation for the Causes of the Saints has substituted for the division into virtues that had hitherto been required. Though this division is retained as an aid, it is not an essential part of the *Positio* or assessment of the servant of God, which is done by means of a documented historical account of his life and of the virtues as these emerge from the account of the life. Newman would surely have approved of this change.

Note

1. See J. Derek Holmes, 'Newman's Reputation and *The Lives of the English Saints*,' *The Catholic Historical Review*, 51 (January 1966), 528–38; and 'John Henry Newman's Attitude towards History and Hagiography,' *Downside Review*, 92 (1974), 86–106.

Conclusion

NEWMAN'S SPIRITUAL theology is firmly anchored in Scripture. Its teachings are drawn from Scripture, and nothing is affirmed without copious quotations from the Bible to support the assertions. Second, certain aspects of it are grounded in patristic thought—especially that of the Greek Fathers. Newman's sermons often breathe their spirit and that spirit is distant from scholastic modes of thinking, being more concrete, more 'practical' to use his terminology. Revealed doctrines are viewed not so much in themselves as in relation to life and action both internal and external. Third, it is a spiritual theology in the Anglican tradition but often presented in relation and contrast to certain contemporary Evangelicals.

Like other spiritualities Newman's contains certain emphases that are distinctive. The first is the recognition that all Christians by reason of their baptism are called to holiness and perfection in their various states of life. His sermons were after all delivered to lay persons. In the Roman Catholic Church it took the Second Vatican Council to remind Catholics of this truth. 'All . . . are called to holiness, according to the Apostle's saying "For this is the will of God, your sanctification."' (1 Thess. 4:3; cf. Eph. 1:4; *Lumen Gentium,* 39) Or again, 'It is therefore clear that all Christians in any state or walk of life are called to the fullness of Christian life and to the perfection of love.' (*Lumen Gentium,* 40)

A century before Bernard Lonergan proposed that conversion is a successive response to God's grace, Newman had come to view it in this way. He linked conversion with God's providence, but he was almost unique in stressing God's personal rather than His universal or general providence.

Newman repeatedly proclaimed worldliness as the great enemy of holiness of life. The world as he understood it meant sin and all the activities of human life and society, legitimate in themselves, but so engrossing the mind, heart, and will of men as to cause them to neglect, or worse, to ignore the primary purpose of life, of growing in sanctity as a preparation for eternal union with God. This darker view of the world, however, is balanced by a brighter sacramental vision of it as leading a Christian to find Christ in all that he does, in all his worldly business and activity, or what St Ignatius called 'contemplation in action.'

Newman placed special emphasis on obedience, self-denial, and detachment from worldly comfort to redress the imbalance of the Evangelicals who preached the necessity of faith to the neglect of the importance of good works. He was also reacting against the 'religion of the day' which, concentrating on the brighter aspects of religion, forgot its darker side.

It is commonly admitted that before the Second Vatican Council Easter and the resurrection had lost their central place in western Christian consciousness. Moreover, theologians treated grace mainly as a quality of the soul, forgetting or undervaluing the doctrine of the indwelling of Christ's Spirit, the Holy Spirit who is the sanctifying agent of the soul. Under the influence of the Eastern Fathers of the Church Newman restored this doctrine to its central place in the Christian revelation and Christian spirituality. The economy of the incarnation, which Newman views as the central doctrine of the Gospels, embraces not merely the Word become man but the atonement and resurrection of Christ who with the Holy Spirit thereafter dwells both in the individual and the Church. Indeed, with the entrance of the Holy Spirit into the individual soul in baptism, the latter is placed in ontic union both with Christ and with the entire mystical body including the saints in heaven. This ontological basis of spirituality and growth in holiness has been reiterated in the Second Vatican Council, which refers to holiness as union with Christ through the action of the Holy Spirit, the Spirit of love and the bond of charity.

Even in his lifetime it was recognized that Newman lived in the invisible world whose reality he tried and succeeded in communicating to others by his words and by the example of his life. That world is inhabited by the Trinity, the risen Christ, Mary body and soul enthroned as queen of heaven, and by all the angels and saints. In true ecumenical fashion he tried to dispel Protestant suspicion of the Church's devotion to Mary. This he did by presenting her as the Second Eve after the manner of the Church Fathers, so that his view was solidly based both dogmatically and theologically but manifested a loving affection without exaggerated piety and gushy emotion.

Prayer, a central element in all spiritualities, was regarded by Newman as a means of communication with the invisible world, but he assigned a special importance to intercessory prayer as binding together the whole Church militant and triumphant.

In presenting Christ as the model and pattern of sanctity Newman focused upon Christ's sufferings and privations, and therefore the role of these in the sanctification of the Christian especially by creating a more intimate union between the soul and Christ and by promoting in the Christian a greater understanding of and sympathy with his fellow beings. Newman's moral portraits of the Old Testament saints are unique, and they are presented not merely as patterns of imitation but as fellow members of the community of saints who can help and sustain us in our spiritual struggles.

Finally, there are two distinctive characteristics of his spirituality which account for its enduring vitality. Reacting against excessive emotions and the attention paid to spiritual 'experiences' on the part of the Evangelicals, Newman took no short cuts to arouse emotions. Such emotions would have no lasting value nor sustain one over a long period of time in the arduous task of striving for holiness. The emotions he arouses are affections based upon ever fresh 'realizations' of the truths of revelation as they touch on one's concrete way of life.

Second, Newman's presentation of spiritual realities stirs the conscience. Consequently, it places the reader in the position in which he has either to accept or reject what has been presented and to choose to act or not upon it. It is impossible to remain neutral. This was the reaction of countless hearers and readers of his sermons and accounts for the continued influence these sermons exercise today. That influence is largely hidden, but the work of the Spirit is a hidden work.

If Newman is eventually declared a doctor of the Church, as Pope Pius XII predicted, it is likely to be not only by reason of his controversial and philosophical writings but also by reason of his vision of the Christian life enshrined in writings that have already become classics of Christian spirituality.